Building Bigger, Busier, and More Profitable Teams

Debbie De Grote

A Guide for Forward Thinking Real Estate Teams and Groups

With Allan Dalton

Anderson-Noble Publishing
Seal Beach, California

Visit our Web site at **www.Excelleum.com** for more information on Debbie De Grote.

Library of Congress Control Number: 2016962898

ISBN: 9781845684050

Published in the United States of America by
Big Guns Marketing, LLC dba
Anderson – Noble Publishing
12340 Seal Beach Blvd., #B632
Seal Beach, CA 90740

Excelleum…When Excellence Matters

This book is available at quantity discounts for bulk purchases.
For information, please call 1-855-420-1400

*To the thousands of
entrepreneurial minded real estate
team leaders and the real estate brokers
who support their efforts
across North America.*

TABLE OF CONTENTS

Forward

Once Upon A Time . . .

Forward thinking real estate professionals dreamt of the day that their individual real estate sales career could be converted into a bonafide real estate business. One employing highly organized systems, services, and team-orientated associates that would lead to income and profits that far exceeded what they could accomplish individually.

Perhaps you have had this dream as well?

Given how many real estate teams or groups are presently thriving, it is clear that the future of real estate teams will not be denied, discouraged, disrupted, or eliminated.

Rather, future real estate teams will become even more prominent, prodigious, and professional.

Not because I say so, but because thousands of highly functioning, profitable, and powerful real estate teams and groups are demanding such.

My motivation for writing this book is two-fold.

First, I want this book to serve as a guide to both highly accomplished and burgeoning future teams, one to reveal proven strategies, services, and operating systems that enable real estate teams and groups to build bigger, busier, and more profitable real estate businesses.

My second motivation is to make it possible for real estate brokers and residential management teams across North America to better understand the deep determination, resolve, and dedication that entrepreneurial team leaders possess, and how real estate brokerages can better leverage real estate teams and groups as a revenue and profit generating resource for their companies.

Over the past 20 years, I have dedicated more than 60,000 private coaching calls to individuals, brokers, brand leaders, and real estate teams. During these coaching sessions, it became apparent early on that my real estate team and group clients encountered a myriad of challenges not faced by my mega producing clients.

Their coaching and consultative needs extended far beyond the personal business planning, networking, marketing, presentation skills, scripting, prospecting, and contact management disciplines.

Instead, my team and group leader clients were in need of coaching strategies and proven systems more similar to my broker clients and business owners of all sizes.

To ensure that this book's content is consistent with its title, *Building Bigger, Busier, and More Profitable Teams*, I will be showcasing a variety of exemplary real estate teams and groups of all sizes.

I hope you enjoy the book and find it most valuable for the successful growth and future of your real estate teams, groups, and brokerages

The Evolution of Real Estate Teams

By Debbie De Grote

People often ask me why Excelleum is so focused on finding new ways to help teams succeed. I suppose the short answer is because teams are a dominant force in the industry and if you ask the majority of agents coming into the business what the vision for their future is, they typically answer, "To someday have a team."

So whether you love them or hate them, apparently teams are here to stay!

Personally, I have another reason for dedicating so much time and focus to helping teams. I was that over worked, over stressed, top producing agent who was producing over 150 closed transactions a year and taking just about the same amount of listings annually. All of this with just a single administrative person to help me.

I made great money, yes!

However, some days I worked 16 hours a day, which is not something you can sustain forever. I am often asked, "Why didn't you build a team?" It's a great question. At the time that I was doing this large amount of personal production, teams did not exist. I was the first agent in my market, and one of the first in the nation, to have a full-time administrative assistant.

I was also one of the first to have a car phone. I found an old magazine the other day, one with a much younger me pictured on the cover, with an article titled, "Car Phone, Tool or Toy?" They interviewed me because I was young and out producing the veterans. They thought it was quite fascinating that I had an administrative assistant and a car phone.

It seems silly that the simple things we are used to today were cutting edge back then. I have no idea why it did not occur to anyone at that time to build a team. I can tell you, though, without a doubt, if a coach had gotten ahold of me then and taught me what we teach our clients now, I could have doubled my production to over 300 units in a year, easily!

Just like many of you, I was a rainmaker and a closer. I had more leads than I could manage, and no one to help me with them. My profit was fine, but my quality of life wasn't great.

That's why I want to help others who are stuck in the same rut that I was find a way to have their cake and eat it too. I want to help top producers build a real business, a business that works even when they aren't working, a business that leverages their time and talent, and a business that they can sell one day and retire on if they choose to. I want them to have a real business and not just a job.

In 1999 I transitioned from personal real estate production to a full time coach and consultant for the real estate industry. Since then my coaching clients have been a who's who of some of the best sales professionals across North America. As Vice President of The Mike Ferry Organization, coach to the coaches at Keller Williams MAPS Coaching, and founder of Excelleum Coaching & Consulting, I have had the opportunity to work with thousands of agents. In the last ten years I would say that more than 70% of my coaching focus has been dedicated to helping top producing agents develop and build their teams. Teams that come in all shapes and sizes, where some are stellar and some are struggling to pull it all together.

I have logged thousands of coaching hours helping brokers and managers work with their teams, build a team-centric culture that provides the services the teams need to grow, and recruit established teams, team leaders, and team members.

Because coaching teams is one of our strengths, together with my faculty of extremely experienced coaches, we have spent countless hours working on new strategies to help our teams and group leaders build bigger, busier, and more profitable teams. We have helped these teams improve their range, reach, and influence in their market. Because as we all know, this business is ever changing and if you are through changing, then you are through.

As I watched our teams struggle to hire, fire, and train their people I wrote the book *The Real Estate Agent's Complete Guide To Hiring, Training, and Retaining Top Talent*, so that they would have a valuable reference book to refer to and for my coaches to work from.

This book contains a wealth of contributions by my team of talented coaches, especially Coach Alyssa Granlund, who helped me turn a rough cut into the valuable tool that it is today. It is also why I enlisted the help of Pete Mitchell to work with Allan Dalton and myself to co-create the Community Marketing System to give them new and better ways to set themselves apart as the experts in the community and the go to for valuable information and advice when buying or selling a home.

So as you can see, we are truly all in when it comes to helping teams thrive.

Due to of all of this, I have had no choice but to naturally analyze the evolution of real estate teams and examine the many shapes and sizes of teams and groups across North America. I realized that their stories would not only be a very valuable addition to this book, but the heart of the book. I know you will enjoy reading the included interviews with industry leaders as much as we enjoyed the process of interviewing them.

I thought it would be appropriate to start our discussion at the beginning by taking a look at the forerunner of today's teams: the twosomes. What is that old saying? "You can't know where you are going unless you know where you have been."

The Real Estate Twosomes

Even though twosomes are not the focus of this book, I felt it was important to mention them. Many of them are running a smooth, profitable, and incredibly successful business without some of the headaches and hassles that developing and managing a large team can bring. Let's examine a few types of twosomes.

Husband and wife twosomes or "spouses selling houses" were probably the first to team up. It made sense, at least in theory. They could work together to juggle kids and a busy career, and keep all of the money in the family.

Next we have the "let's team up" twosomes who spring up because they are friends or office acquaintances. Just like the husband and wife teams, it might make sense to divide and conquer. They also, potentially, look to leave the duties they don't want to do to their team member, and maybe even have an occasional day off. Many of these twosomes feel that two agents for the price of one will give them a competitive edge in their market when competing for business.

Then we have the mother and son, father and daughter, etc. family twosomes that often form when the children who grew up around the business, admiring their parent's successes and seeing the opportunity the industry offers, decide to join them.

While some of these twosomes prove to be very successful, many of them, for the most part, produce modest results. Why? It's simple. Too many of them were formed out of identified weaknesses rather than synergistic strengths. In other words, one of the parties said, "Hey Bob, I don't like to prospect and you do, you don't like to do paperwork and I do, let's team up!"

Whatever the size of your team or the size of the team you hope to build in the future, you need a plan and a strategy. You must give careful thought to who you invite to join you and how you define the roles and responsibilities of the team members if you expect it to function like a well-oiled machine.

Top talent always attracts a following, so it's common for a top producing agent to have someone organically come up to them and say, "I want to be on your team." What is also common is that the top producer says, "Sure." Now they have a team that they don't know what to do with, and most likely the person who just joined their team isn't necessarily a perfect fit.

This is why many teams fail. What's even worse than the team failing is that it often pulls the top producer completely off their game and his or her production crashes.

As I write this, I am reminded of just such a top producer. This top producer is only about four years into the business but he is killing it, doing over $60 million in production as an individual agent. He is in a $1-5 million average home price market, so it's easy for him to manage the units with just an admin to assist.

One day someone said to him, "I should join your team!" Then along came another, and another. He called me for help and said, "I now have eight people on my team and I have no idea what to do with them. They are not producing, my business is down by 50%, and I am stressed out, help me!"

I had him come to the office with his team and it was almost comical to watch him walking across the parking lot with eight of them following behind like baby ducklings. After having each of them complete a DISC analysis and helping him create a plan, we discovered all but two of them needed to be fired. We kept the admin and one strong buyer agent, which is all he needs for now.

With his admin we are working on systems and structure, with his buyer agent we are working on skills and accountability, and the team leader himself is focused on the over one million dollar listings. He is now back on track and all is well.

Thank goodness he called me!

In the book *Good to Great* Jim Collins says, "You need to get the right people on the bus and then you need to get them in the right seat." This is critical if you wish to build a happy and productive business. I hope as you read the stories of the great teams in this book you will be encouraged to take it slow, be methodical, and learn from their lessons.

Before you make your first hire, have a plan and consider reaching out to a coach to help you build out your plan and create the vision for your future.

At Excelleum we believe that no two agents, teams, or brands are alike and that is why I want you to understand that I did not write this book to encourage everyone who reads it to build a team, nor do I seek to admonish brokers who have chosen not to be team-centric. Instead, I hope it will provide you with valuable insights and information from some of the best in the industry that will then allow you to make your own informed decision about what is right for your career path. Once you define your vision, if you choose to engage us the coaches at Excelleum would be delighted to coach you to achieve it.

One of the aspects I love most about the real estate business is that success comes in all shapes and sizes, and as you read the interviews included in this book you will see how different and unique each of the interviewees are. They do, however, share something that shines through: their passion for the industry and the part they play in it. I, for one, applaud and so appreciate their passion. It is what inspires the coaches and me to do what we do.

Real Estate Consolidation Sparked the Development of Large Teams and Groups

As I was preparing to write this book, I read an article that sparked a realization. The article said that as recent as five decades ago, nearly

95% of all real estate brokerages in North America had ten or fewer real estate agents working for them.

What does this have to do with the evolution of teams? My answer is everything!

As I read this article my realization was this: back in the day when a real estate agent came to a point in their career where they believed they had developed the skills and ability to take their business to the next level, when they had an entrepreneurial yearning to build something bigger and better than they could do on their own by just doing one deal at a time, there was an obvious career path available to them. As I shared earlier, it's a feeling I understand all too well.

The path at that time was to start their own, usually small, real estate firm. They knew if they opened up shop they could do their own personal production and keep all of the profit, hire a few agents who would cover the overhead of the office, and maybe even put a little extra profit from the agents' production in their pocket. Because of this, mom and pop shops started showing up on every corner.

The consolidation that has occurred in the real estate industry, which has produced mega companies with mega muscle in the marketplace, made this no longer a viable and profitable option for the budding entrepreneurs. However, their talent and energy to grow could not be stopped, so they had to find another way, and they were faced with only two choices.

1) If their broker was supportive of teams, build a real estate team or group within their present company.
2) If their broker wasn't team friendly, join a company that was, and build their team there.

Ironically, the success of their broker and other real estate companies was now inadvertently blocking the inevitable personal evolution of successful agents who were looking to grow by building their own real estate company.

The message these successful agents often received from their broker is, "It's going to be too hard to start your own company and compete against me and other large brokers who dominate the area, and I won't allow you to disrupt my company, culture, or brand by developing your own company within my company."

Something had to give. And it did.

How the Change Began to Take Place

Forward thinking brokers began to understand that they would lose their top producers and the teams these top producers now led if they blocked their growth and success.

They also knew that top producers are generally their top listing agents, and listings generate market share and quality buyer leads that the entire company benefits from.

They realized that if they were going to allow teams, they had to become more effective at negotiating compensation plans that would allow them to keep and support their teams, while at the same time making possible for the teams to attract team members with fair splits and opportunities for growth.

The dilemma became that if they did not allow these top producers to bring new agents onboard under their name and current split, there would not be enough profit to allow them to attract talent to their teams.

That is why you will often see brokers allowing a top producer to close the deals and collect the commissions based on their higher splits, and then cut their salespeople on the team a check for 50% of their profits. This policy may, of course, vary due to services the company provides and other unique factors.

Naturally, brokers do not love the fact that this gives them a much smaller piece of the new agent's production than they would have if the new agent closed these deals on their own at a lower new agent split.

However, most brokers justify the decision by believing that if the agent stood on their own, they would most likely do fewer deals than they could potentially produce as a member of a viable team.

Many brokers both then and now have a firm policy that you cannot recruit from within. This ensures the teams will scout their talent from outside the company and will bring even more new talent and profit, albeit a smaller share, to the company roster. Then if one day agents leave the team, they would have the opportunity to stay with the company as an individual agent.

There are even team-centric brokers who assist their agents with recruiting by testing and assessing new agent hires to see if they might potentially benefit more by joining a team versus being a single agent, and then gently direct them toward the appropriate team.

These brokers are also realizing that if they are truly going to get on board with these teams, they must define extremely clear policies and procedures, such as:

- How team members are recruited
- The initial training they must complete
- How team agreements are structured
- Compensation models for the various roles
- Accounting services
- Training team leaders to lead effectively
- Tools and technology for the teams to manage their lead pipelines
- Resolution of team conflicts
- Final veto power when teams are hiring new members
- Office space allotted to the team
- Other fees per member they feel necessary to make the numbers make sense

If you are a broker and do not know where to begin when it comes to putting your team policies in place, reach out and I will connect you to one of our team coaches who can help. I would encourage you to do this sooner rather than later, because I can assure you that you don't want to have multiple teams on different plans. It will create dissension and can cause you to lose a quality team who feels slighted because their deal is not as good as the next guy's.

Also, if you are insisting that teams work predominately with the company affiliates and services then you need to introduce them to the team members early on and ask the affiliates to help you train the new members and build a relationship with them from the beginning.

More on Compensation

I am not going to spend too much time or detail on how team members are compensated because, as has already been established, they are all unique. I do address some of these questions in *The Real Estate Agent's Complete Guide to Hiring, Training, and Retaining Top Talent.*

It is common that buyer agents are paid anywhere from 35-50%, depending on how the lead is generated, how much it costs per lead, and what support services to close the lead are provided.

Listing partners to the team leader may earn 25-35% from each listing and will, of course, be expected to handle most of the service aspects when managing a listing.

If they are a true listing specialist who goes out on their own, takes and manages the listing and the negotiations, they will usually start out on a 50/50 split.

Some teams employ new agents to open the doors on behalf of the buyer agents who are showing the property. They will often receive 5% or 10% of the commission or a flat fee per deal, depending on the price range. These showing assistants typically do nothing but open the doors and demonstrate, and then the buyer agent closes them.

Teams who often carry 50 or more listings may pay a more experienced member of the team to oversee some of the seller service, such as opening the doors to high end listings for buyers and agents and making sure the homes are shown properly. In the high end market it's common again to see an override for this to be 5-10%.

Some teams will allow team members to submit a roster of their friends and family so that a slightly higher split, potentially 10% more, will be paid if they do a deal with a team member.

Teams also need to make the decision as to whether they allow all team members to list and work with buyers or separate these positions.

Of course, each team will need to evaluate what they pay for leads, if anything, and how they provide them. They must decide on the services they provide to the members inside of their team. For example, do they split marketing costs with them? They will also need to think about experience level and what that team member brings to the table.

All of this goes into making the decision as to how to structure your split agreements. This goes to show how each team situation and compensation structure is unique.

I would advise team leaders, just as I advise brokers, to have clear compensation models, expectations, and job descriptions in writing, because when you pay everyone on a different model of split, problems are very easily created.

You'll want to avoid making on-the-fly, one off split deals, as this often results in confusion and disagreement. In fact, don't make any split arrangements or any type of compensation agreements without thinking it through carefully.

Think it through, do the math, put it in writing, and be sure it's clear and still profitable for you!

Real Estate Team Evolution within Brands

Brands that did not participate in brokerage splits, but instead only on gross commission income of the firm, recognized that their play was to:

1) Create a big enough international brand, one that allowed brokerages to compete against large local consolidated brands.
2) Since the profits of brands have nothing to do with how their franchise brokerages manage internal commission splits, recognize that it was to their advantage to foster a culture based upon catering to top producers who wished to develop teams. After all, what better way could there be to recruit top producers?

As you look back in time and see all of the change that has occurred, you can understand why the evolution of teams has left the industry in a structural battle.

The participants:

- Certain brands, as mentioned, have seized a revenue generating opportunity by becoming the perceived meccas for real estate teams.
- Brands that remain essentially indifferent on the subject of teams.
- Brands that do not encourage or promote the growth of teams. Although many will allow them to exist within the company culture as long as they play by the rules dictated and the return to the broker is enough to justify their existence.

Most large and successful brokers recognize that, like it or not, the trend towards real estate teams and groups is here to stay. Many brokers are now starting to realize that they must balance real estate team related compensation models by doing the following.

First, by better quantifying their real estate teams. This includes the value of their greater brand, their market share, marketing and technological resources, and physical locations.

Second, by recognizing that their real estate teams, if properly integrated, can absorb for the brokerage, as a byproduct of their need to provide specialized and differentiated team services, the following expenses: recruiting costs, management overhead, marketing costs, and training costs.

With the growth of mega companies and mega offices, the task of a manager training 100 or more agents is challenging at best. Teams provide a way for them to shift some of the burden of training and mentoring new agents and developing rising talent to the team leaders.

I encourage team leaders to never lose sight of all that their brokers and owners do to provide them with the opportunity to flourish as a meaningful part of the operation. When the team leader shows respect for the brand, the broker, and the company culture, their team members are more likely to respect the team leader. When all parties work together in an environment of respect and appreciation you have the ultimate and most unbeatable form of teamwork possible.

That's my take on the evolution of brands. Regarding the future, however, that's in the hands of us all. And as we know, it's ever changing and evolving!

As we close this chapter I would like to say once again on behalf of everyone on my excellent Excelleum team, that at Excelleum we do not favor any particular type of team. We do not believe that every agent should become a team or group, nor do we favor a particular brand. Instead, we favor and respect the clients who choose to allow us to help them be all that they can be. We value and appreciate you and celebrate your success, the best for you is yet to come!

A $400 Million Team
that Continues to Grow

An interview with Phil Malamatenios

Debbie De Grote: Phil, is it safe to say that you, for the most part, co-manage Stanfield Real Estate while Sean leads it?

Phil Malamatenios: Yes, that would be a good description, but it might be even more accurate to say that while Sean leads the team and I manage it, we have many others with great skill sets. We strive to put everybody to their highest and best use.

DD: Can you break that down for me?

PM: Sean is the visionary, leader, and essence of the team. He expects me to be the glue to ensure that our culture and the way it is managed are consistent with his vision, ethics, integrity, and overall admirable business principles. This allows Sean to focus most on his incomparable value, that being creating and serving real estate clients. By involving all team members and allowing them to focus on their unique skills, the beneficiary is always the client.

DD: I agree with your description of Sean, who I am proud to have as a client. So let me ask you, now that you've mentioned where his focus is, what is yours?

PM: I allow Sean to focus on what is the best and highest use of his time by relieving him of as many of the day to day operational challenges that occur within our organization as possible. This means ensuring that our team members and their administrative and career developmental needs are professionally and consistently responded to.

DD: I am sure that our readers would first and foremost want to know more about Sean himself. What can you share with us about what makes Sean Stanfield the remarkably successful real estate leader that he is?

PM: Well Sean, interestingly just as yourself, Debbie, has been in real estate since age 18. He started with ERA and then joined a company that I know you are very familiar with, that being First Team. He remained with First Team for 25 years.

DD: Why don't you tell us where he ranked out of the thousands of agents who were also there at First Team?

PM: To the best of my recollection, and he would never be one to dwell on this, he was number one in the company for approximately 16 or 17 years running.

DD: There is nothing I respect more from all that my clients do, than consistent excellence, which Sean embodies. When did he make the transition from being a top producer to developing a real estate team?

PM: It was around the real estate boom of 2003 to 2005 or so, when he concluded that after regularly working 18 to 20 hour days he needed to delegate. He also recognized that he had developed immense personal brand value due to his success and stellar reputation both inside and outside of the real estate community. And this was the time for him to leverage his considerable accomplishments by forming a team.

DD: Who did he hire first?

PM: His first hire was long before branding his team; he had a personal assistant going back to 1998. After that, his first hire was his sister and she was among the first who provided Sean with assistance. She would open properties, show clients properties, that sort of thing. This was after he first hired a transaction coordinator. Sean went along with transaction coordinators and his sister, and then I came along in the fall of 2007.

DD: What was your background Phil?

PM: Well, essentially my entire professional life has been in real estate, but I started in a marketing capacity for Coast Newport Properties in Newport Beach.

DD: I remember that company had three upscale offices in and around Newport Beach. Did they bring you in to take their marketing to a higher level?

PM: They actually brought me in to just do the marketing basics. That being direct mail, etc. But I evolved that position to where I was strategically responsible for developing their overall marketing, and eventually became Director of Marketing.

DD: In a sense you just applied your intelligence and work ethic to that company's needs. Is that what you have brought to Sean's team?

PM: Yes, but in addition, Sean saw my background in the upscale communities through my years at Coast Newport as a match for his clientele and as a marketing bridge to serving additional higher end communities. These are communities which he now dominates. Nobody, and I mean nobody, in real estate is more of a natural marketing person than Sean. It was inevitable therefore that Sean would connect with these upscale communities. Sean also felt it was important to be connected to a brand that had that same upscale approach to marketing and servicing our elite clientele.

DD: Is it safe to say that the combination of your background and Sean's insistence on first class service has brought a new elegance to how your team serves the home buyers and sellers in your community?

PM: Yes, that is well put. Sean is steadfast in raising the bar in all facets of real estate.

DD: What other changes did Sean oversee regarding marketing?

PM: Sean recognized early on, and I think you may have helped him with this as our team's coach, that he had to transform his brand from Sean Stanfield the person, to Sean Stanfield the team.

DD: So, keeping with our Orange County location, Sean knew he had to evolve from being Walt Disney to creating Disneyland.

PM: Indeed. Sean knew that for all of his teammates to excel and maximize their potential as salespeople, the brand equity had to be built into the word group versus the name Sean Stanfield. Thus, Stanfield Real Estate.

DD: Phil, I can feel your pride in Sean, the group, and the team members. It is palpable. Tell me about how the group functions.

PM: Well we have approximately 20 salespeople, with three or four at any one time working exclusively as buyer agents. We encourage our team members to work with both sellers and buyers and to do their own prospecting. We are constantly working with everyone on their professional skill development, business planning, contact management, etc. And, of course, our commitment to our team members is to provide them with the best in coaching, which you and your varied faculty deliver us.

DD: What percentage of your buyer leads as a group do you believe are generated specifically from your listings?

PM: At least 50%.

DD: Phil, do you completely just serve the needs of the entire group, or do you also compete for listings?

PM: No, Sean told me from day one that I was to serve as a resource to everyone else on the team. Consequently, my focus is helping team members do more business.

DD: Let's say an important group policy goes out to the group. Is it from you or Sean?

PM: More likely from me, but Sean is included if necessary.

DD: How about group meetings. How often and who runs them?

PM: We meet once a week and sometimes Sean runs them, other times I will. As a coach, I think you understand that people thrive when they hear a variety of voices. Just as you have multiple coaches working with us, I think the team likes to have multiple voices lead the meetings.

DD: Why do you think Sean decided to name his organization Stanfield Real Estate rather than using the word team or group?

PM: Our goal as previously stated is to raise the bar. Everybody is a team or group, we want to be a firm. We are experts and want to be viewed as professionals similar to a law firm, CPA firm, or consulting firm.

DD: Why, after 25 years of working at First Team Real Estate, a large independent brand, did Sean decide to make a change in companies?

PM: Sean concluded that since he was providing the training, the coaching, and the marketing, that all he was looking for was the best brand to represent his clientele. The sign that our clients put in their yard creates a feel of what you can expect to see inside. We want our brand to represent our clients.

DD: How do you feel about the future of teams and individual agents?

PM: I am often amazed at how some agents can even survive without being on a team. In fact, I believe with each passing year it will become even more difficult to succeed without building a team.

DD: What else makes you feel this strongly about the future of real estate teams in terms of absolute dominance?

PM: Well, just go visit a lot of real estate offices and you will find 5-6,000 square feet locations and there will be three people there and no customers. Come visit our office and you will see 20 people working arduously in 1,200 square feet. That's a major difference between teams and non-team offices.

DD: That is a brilliant observation Phil.

PM: Let me build upon it. I have no research to back this up, yet from my experience I have observed that members of teams and groups unite and socialize more than individually performing agents. Non team agents are more likely to come to the following conclusion, one which is harmful to their careers: why don't I just work at home more? This begins a spiral of inactivity and work avoidance. When someone is on a team they become energized and synergized by seeing other team members working and constantly discussing properties, buyer needs, and strategies with one another.

DD: Wonderful explanation Phil. If your team members had to decide between staying with your current brand as an individual agent, or staying a part of Stanfield Real Estate, what would their choice be?

PM: I can't look into their minds, but I believe if they could only have one of the two, everyone would 100% select Stanfield Real Estate. But fortunately, they do not have to decide because they have the best of both worlds. Plus, because our group is so relentless in how we analyze all of our resources from both the group and our brand, I think we probably do the best job of leveraging our brand as well, especially versus individual agents.

DD: I know you do, since one of our coaching sessions with your group was you inviting one of our Excelleum faculty members to facilitate a meeting on how to best leverage the Stanfield brand and the corporate brand during listing presentations. What's most amazing, however, is how much business your group does. I would like you to share what the results are.

PM: In 2015, our group produced just over $400 million in production.

DD: Indeed you are always listed in the top ten of *Real Trends'* top teams, which is showcased in the *Wall Street Journal*. How significant is that recognition?

PM: It not only is a credential we consistently leverage, but our entire group, and rightfully so, basks in the pride of knowing that we consistently rank within the top ten of all North American real estate teams. We like to say that means nothing to our clients unless we perform for them, but our success is proof that our model works.

DD: Do you do the recruiting?

PM: We select more than we recruit. We get calls every single day from agents seeking to join our team. I never saw this happen to any degree at a regular real estate office. We are not looking to have 1,000 agents. We are looking to quadruple our business, but not by quadrupling the size of our team. Another reason why we don't hire a lot of experienced agents who contact us is that many, although they do far less business that Sean, display a much bigger ego. In fact, Sean is more modest than anyone of his level of success that I have ever seen in real estate.

DD: When you do hire someone, what is the selection process?

PM: Well Debbie, one of the reasons you are our team coach is that you not only do our behavioral assessments, but more than anyone else I know of who coaches, the foundation of your coaching begins with these professional assessments. Therefore, if someone we interview is revealed not to be prospecting oriented, this can be a disqualifier. Sean is looking for agents who don't have giant egos and understand success comes from hard work.

DD: Phil, when the California market went into a significant recession years ago, was Stanfield Real Estate, because of its size, more nimble than larger companies?

PM: Absolutely. Sean led a major and highly sophisticated prospecting, marketing, administrative, and sales effort towards representing REO departments and short sale bank administrators, along with campaigns directed to buyers and homeowners of distressed properties. These comprehensive efforts continue to this day. I cannot give you all of the details out of respect for our group, but the answer is we were both nimble and Sean was visionary.

DD: Are there members of Stanfield Real Estate that work out of offices other than the group's main office?

PM: Yes, we have office space in many different offices throughout Southern California that many agents will work out of. Still, most prefer the synergy of working out of our main location. As I mentioned earlier, agents like to feel the energy around them.

DD: I want to give you my summary of what you have said Phil, and what I know about your group, to see if you agree. Unlike some teams, where there are people who assume different tasks all geared to helping the rainmaker do more personal business, Sean and you have structured Stanfield Real Estate as a way to give everyone else better credentials, better marketing, and better coaching. In this way, you are building a bigger, busier, and better business.

PM: I could not have said it better, precisely.

DD: Thank you Phil and congratulations to Sean and each and every member of Stanfield Real Estate.

The Team that's 'Vacuuming Up' Center City Philly's Real Estate Market

An interview with Mike McCann

Allan Dalton: Mike, when and how did you decide to enter the real estate business?

Mike McCann: In June of 1986, a couple of friends of mine were taking real estate classes and they told me that I should take the course. Within three minutes I came to the conclusion, "Oh My God, this is what I want to do."

AD: Wow, passion from the outset! What had you done before this epiphany?

MM: I was in the restaurant business at a hotel doing room service, being a banquet waiter, and providing coffee service. But of greater significance, in terms of preparing me for real estate, was my experience selling Kirby vacuum cleaners door to door for a period of three and a half years.

AD: What was that experience like in general?

MM: I was very successful. So much so that early on I opened up my own business. My success didn't take me where I wanted to get to, so I proceeded to go back to the restaurant business.

AD: Mike, how much did your background in both door to door vacuum cleaner sales and all facets of the hotel and restaurant sectors influence your success in real estate?

MM: Big time. Regarding having a service sector background and specifically the restaurant business, I must say that I think anyone who wants to flourish in real estate would be well served by first experiencing all that working for, or that actually running, a restaurant demands.

AD: How so?

MM: It teaches a person how to operate efficiently, how to present yourself, the importance of patience and tolerance with people, and a better understanding of the human condition. And what better preparation is there regarding pace and pressure? This "must perform" atmosphere is similar to a high paced, high functioning real estate office, especially when in a bustling urban market such as my beloved Philadelphia.

AD: Let's move now to your early career.

MM: Of greatest significance was at the very beginning of my career when one of my friends announced to me, "Mike you need to go to work for my buddy." His buddy was a property manager and was not involved in sales. Therefore, I would go to this real estate office and they don't even do sales, and think to myself, "What's this all about?" Well, I guess if you believe that necessity is the mother of invention then this was my situation. I had to completely teach myself everything about selling real estate, and this was before the internet.

AD: Then how did you teach yourself?

MM: I quickly got my hands on every book and every tape produced by the National Association of Realtors©, and my Pennsylvania Board of Realtors as well. Fortunately, I hadn't left my hotel job, so I had the means to pay for my real estate apprenticeship along with my real estate tuition.

AD: Sounds like you were quite busy back then, just as you are today.

MM: I would start at the hotel at 6 am, and would leave at about 10:30 and head into the real estate office.

AD: I thought only Rocky was up running around the streets of Philly at that time of the morning! But seriously, how long were you doing two full time jobs?

MM: Fortunately, within three years I was number one in real estate sales for all of Philadelphia and produced 90 sales without a team in 1988.

AD: What section of Philadelphia did you zero in on?

MM: Downtown Philadelphia, which is a half mile from Independence Hall. We are an urban environment, known for our Row homes, condos, and low rises. While we have a busy business district, there are plenty of residences all throughout our Center City Philadelphia.

AD: Great city indeed, my daughter is a graduate of U Penn, so I have visited numerous times. But Mike, not everyone who brought room service and sold vacuums becomes number one in the City of Brotherly Love. What was it about you, that you very early on in your career proved yourself to be this real estate force of nature?

MM: Although I spend my time looking forwards and not backwards, when I do reflect upon my background and its role in my achievements, I cannot overlook the role of one of my mentors. His name was James B. Marion, III. He taught me everything about sales. I was selling $644 vacuum cleaners in the middle of a gas crisis with interest rates of 21% back in 1979 and 1980. This is only because he taught me tenacity and basically told me, "Mike. Never ever ever give up."

AD: Tell me more about this person's influence on you.

MM: He was the greatest man in the world to me. He was a first generation Jewish immigrant, his parents were poor and from Germany. He not only went to college, but was getting his law degree and sold vacuum cleaners to make enough money for law school. He ended up with multiple franchises, owning an estate with an airplane and a home with a tennis court in Florida. While it was so difficult to get jobs back in 1979, even at McDonald's, he told me that at this job that the harder I worked the more I could make. This was music to my ears as, since I was a teenager, I used to say to my dear mother, "Mom, I wish I could find a job that would pay more for working harder, because I always work harder than everyone else!"

AD: You seem to have always been inspired. How does that manifest itself these days when it comes to inspiring others?

MM: Every day, beginning in the morning, I am singing songs and shouting out sayings I learned from James B. Marion, III.

AD: Let's now turn to the origins of your legendary real estate team.

MM: So by the 1980s I am doing 90 transactions a year. This is with no internet, no transaction coordinators, and no buyers' agents, nothing. My wife observed how I was working. Now my wife has the brain of an engineer and my brain is one of a sales guy, so when she volunteered to organize me it transformed my business and my real estate future.

AD: How did she begin to introduce her organizational acumen into your business?

MM: Like this: "Okay Mike, when you get an Agreement of Sale, walk me through everything that is required to bring the transaction to closing and post-closing, and I will develop an administrative system. Now let's review everything you do from the point of securing a listing agreement, so I can create standardized checklists and processes for this as well."

AD: What impact did this have on your career specifically?

MM: Because my wife organized my business, it now enabled me to hire an assistant. Had she not organized me, I would not have been sufficiently organized to even hire an assistant. But now there was some order backing up my hurricane-like sales activity.

AD: Which company were you working with back then?

MM: Steve M. Glass Real Estate, an independent family brokerage. There were only four people in the place.

AD: Did you do rentals, given your urban marketplace?

MM: I did rentals for the first six months to help generate instant income. But there is not much money in rentals, although it is a great way to develop real estate people skills. And it pays the bills for new Realtors before they do sales.

AD: Let's continue with your next hires and growth.

MM: By 1992 I hired my next assistant, and with good reason. I had made another $70,000 due to my first assistant, who I paid $25,000 those 30 or so years ago. I concluded that I was now ready to hire more help and colleagues, and this was long before there were so called real estate teams, at least in Philadelphia.

AD: How did you attract other salespeople?

MM: Due to my amount of personal business, I put my company on the map. Reporters started to view me as the trusted source for all things real estate in Downtown Philadelphia. Therefore, I was receiving free publicity and fanfare in my market, and other agents started to take notice.

AD: How did this benefit your overall company?

MM: Sadly, my company began to suffer for personal reasons, and I knew then that this atmosphere was one which would only hurt the growth of my business. Since Prudential Real Estate had been courting me for some time, I decided to leave for Prudential.

AD: How many offices did they have at that time?

MM: Approximately 40 when Fox and Roach, a longstanding Philadelphia institution, bought our Prudential company, Prudential Preferred Properties.

AD: How did that impact you?

MM: I loved their sophistication, their management, their resources, and their willingness to invest in their people. I already was being called Mr. IBM because when I joined their office of 40 agents where they only had one computer at that time, I brought in my own two computers. During this period, unlike most of the other agents in and around Philly, I attended virtually every real estate convention and seminar I could. In fact, I had a website back in 1992, even before Prudential had one.

AD: This is impressive!

MM: Actually, there was only one other person in Philadelphia who also was connected to the best thoughts available throughout the entire industry, and that would be Allan Domb.

AD: You mean the legendary Condo King?

MM: There you go.

AD: Well, you have been with two very prominent brands, Prudential and now Berkshire Hathaway HomeServices. How have you built your personal brand?

MM: That would be through my slogan: Mike McCann, "The Real Estate Man."

AD: That certainly says it all.

MM: Plus that slogan has been plastered all over signs and ads throughout my market.

AD: How does the BHHS brand help you?

MM: It helps me sell more expensive homes.

AD: What is your average price?

MM: My average is around $500,000. In fact, Philly is booming. The more gritty urban neighborhoods that were once frowned upon are now creating bidding wars for homes in the several hundred thousand dollar range. When I started in real estate, it seemed as though everyone wanted to move to the suburbs. Well, now everyone seems to want to move back to town. I guess my team and I were ahead of our time, because we always knew downtown was the only place to be! And because of my background knocking on doors selling vacuum cleaners, I could not be in a better place.

AD: How do you secure your listings?

MM: I send out 9,000 mailings every other month with a CMA report regarding their local neighborhood. But my greatest source is all of the local listing and buying referrals generated from my many years of serving the local community.

AD: How many people are now on your team?

MM: I am blessed with seven full time assistants, two conveyancers, and 18 full time agents.

AD: Do the 18 full time agents work with both buyers and sellers?

MM: Four do a lot of listings, and the rest essentially serve as my buyer specialists.

AD: How do you feed, if you will, these team members with enough buyer leads?

MM: I invest heavily into the major real estate portals for premier placement and referrals, and of course, all of our listings and open houses keep everyone busy.

AD: Do you hope to generate more listing agents as you continue to grow?

MM: As my team members evolve, the goal is for them to become listing agents, and then hire new agents to take their place as buyer agents.
AD: Has hiring become even easier given your growing prominence?

MM: Allan, I could hire 80 existing agents for my team if I were just trying to build a huge team. I get up to ten requests a month from experienced agents asking to join my team. What I do is send them over to management, because I believe so much in Berkshire Hathaway HomeServices Fox and Roach. If I get to the point where my team cannot handle all of our business, I will then hire more team members. But doing so without diluting the earning power of my team members is sacred to me.

AD: What do your seven assistants do?

MM: Prepare agreements, set up appointments, order signs, and order photos. They all follow the checklist that my wife developed as the foundation. I also have a marketing director who places all my ads, does my mailings, decides which properties we feature and where, and also does my mailings, flyers and brochures. Every property I sell generates a postcard and a targeted mailing list. Another assistant handles all correspondence. Allan, I am the whole package, and I have assistance all the way because I provide complete full service for my clients, from painting, to staging, you name it.

AD: How long on average do your people stay with you?

MM: They seem to be McCann Team lifers. One has been with me for 16 years and others for 14 and 12 years. My people don't leave me because they know, figuratively speaking, that I do not leave them.

AD: How about the tenure of your agents?

MM: Lifers as well. How about 16, 15, and 12 years, and a group with ten years or so? They stay because they would rather make more money from a smaller cut, than less money from a bigger cut. We call it the "Mike McCann 1 plus 1 equals 3 system."

AD: The agents you hire, are they mostly new or experienced?

MM: With few exceptions, I opt for new yet highly promising
agents. This is because it would take me more time to purge experienced
agents of their bad habits than it will to train promising new
professionals into the Mike McCann team culture.

AD: How has the building of a team influenced your personal life?

MM: I hired my first buyer specialist in 1996, and I will tell you why. I
decided I was not going to die working 120 hours a week. I craved being
able to spend my Saturdays going to the soccer, football, and
cheerleading activities of my children. After all, the entire motivation
driving my work was to provide for my family. But the rigors of real
estate, when not better organized, was depriving my family of the most
important provision - the attention of both parents.

Therefore, when buyer leads came in, I could now send a message to my
buyer's agent. My first buyer agent freed up my Saturdays, and my next
freed up my Sundays. My real estate team, which is why I love them
dearly, has made it possible for me since the year 2000, to come home on
Friday night and not work at all till Monday morning, except
online. Just like most Philadelphia executives. All Realtors are
executives, but most need to execute differently.

AD: You mention your children, are they part of the business?

MM: They are a big part that gets bigger every day. We have a son and
a younger daughter in the business, Ryan and Julianne. Julianne is
already a top assistant and Ryan, her older brother, is being a force in all
aspects of real estate.

AD: Does anyone on your team do teleprospecting for the team?

MM: Although we have one assistant identifying and mailing expireds
every day, I leave the prospecting to our individual team member
agents.

AD: Do you assign team members geographical areas?

MM: No, the whole market is open to them. That said, with certain
leads I will direct to team members who have displayed greater
knowledge and success pertaining to a particular market.

AD: How many open houses do you conduct on average?

MM: On average we do 50 to 60 open houses each Sunday.

AD: How do you get 18 agents to hold 60 open houses?

MM: I involve a number of agents who are not even on my team to host my open houses. In fact, I received a thank you note from an agent outside of our team where he wrote, "Thanks for helping me sell another $5 million through your open house. Mike, you are The Real Estate Man!" I got a big kick out of that.

AD: From my years at Realtor.com I was involved in meetings with your leader, Larry Flick. He is as smart as they come. What is your relationship with Larry?

MM: I have always respected company leaders. It was Craig Millard with Prudential Preferred who convinced me that it made more sense for me to build a team versus going up against larger real estate companies if I started my own company. And now I learn so much from just watching the amazing leadership and business intelligence that Larry Flick represents. I want to lead my team in the same professional manner that Larry and Joan Docktor lead their team, that team being the entire company.

AD: How often does the team meet in its entirety?

MM: We only meet four times a year at most.

AD: Why not more frequently?

MM: It's simple, we are all too busy. Plus, I am touching everyone, every day, with emails, voice messages, walking around with my singing and slogans, etc. They also know I welcome their calls. If you hire hungry entrepreneurs, you don't have to keep motivating them. They will follow your example.

AD: Mike, tell me about your website.

MM: I use Jim Marks from Virtual Results, and it is world class. I enjoy high SEO. While we will never be Zillow or Realtor.com, we are way up there in our class. I invite your reader to visit and let it speak for itself, but rest assured we show it off to prospective clients. We also maintain a strong presence throughout social media. I get a significant amount of agent referrals because of my blog and usage of Facebook.

AD: Speaking of being a top producer, how much did your team do last year?

MM: We did 794 transactions and $260 million. We usually rank either first or second within all of Berkshire Hathaway HomeServices.

AD: So you are with a brand that has number one market share in Philly, Berkshire Hathaway HomeServices Fox and Roach, you are the number one team, and you are Mike McCann "The Real Estate Man." How can anyone say no to that?

MM: Forgive me for sounding self-praiseworthy, but few do!

AD: Mike, does your world of real estate include personally investing in real estate?

MM: Absolutely! I always tell my agents that depending on the market, I want them to earn another $20,000 to $200,000 extra per year in flipping real estate.

AD: In other words Mike, you seem to take a very personal concern in the financial wellbeing of everybody on your team, and you encourage them to participate in the real estate growth of the inner city.

MM: Absolutely, and I teach long term as well. I want them to buy one or two properties a year so that when they are my age, 55, they have 25 or more paid off properties. In fact, my 26 year old son, who has been with me for four years since graduating from Penn State, already owns seven properties. Allan, it's part of hiring people for life. I have 35 year old guys making hundreds of thousands of dollars, and they leverage me by saying, "Hi, I am the listing/marketing specialist for Mike McCann." It's all about loyalty. I am with Larry and Joan because there are not any brokers in America more loyal to their agents and teams than they are.

AD: You mention how your company is loyal to teams. Why do you think this is so?

MM: Because they are intelligent and care about people. They know you cannot have one manager developing 100 agents, and because of this, good people leave within six months.

AD: Mike, let me end our interview by referencing someone else who is profiled in Debbie De Grote's book. That would be Gino Blefari, the CEO of Berkshire Hathaway HomeServices. I interviewed Gino as well and I am struck with many of your similarities. Have you met Gino?

MM: It's funny you mention that. I did meet Gino, and was so impressed with him and how professionally he presents himself, including his elegance in dressing. I point this out Allan, because everything I do, I want it to reflect well on our profession. I think all of us who make a good living from the real estate industry should always keep in mind how important it is that we represent our companies, our teams, and ourselves.

AD: Thank you so much Mike.

Teaming Up with Local Merchants

An interview with Julie Vanderblue

Allan Dalton: Julie, what is the name of your organization?

Julie Vanderblue: Branding is very important to me and therefore, I have approached the subject with great care. For starters, I am the president of The Higgins Group, and we are a Christie's affiliate. Rick Higgins is the founder, broker, and CEO of the company. Within this framework I am also the president of Vanderblue Associates and the President of The Vanderblue Team.

AD: Please walk me through this branding complexity.

JV: Rick Higgins early on identified me as an executive who could help him grow The Higgins Group. We now have 14 offices throughout Fairfield County, Connecticut. He believed, and I agreed, that having me help with company recruiting, training, leadership, and overall growth would be mutually beneficial, and it has been.

AD: How does this coincide with your other titles and responsibilities?

JV: The next title, President of Vanderblue Associates, is the name that oversees my own Vanderblue Team, and smaller teams which decide to work under the umbrella of Vanderblue Associates. Vanderblue Associates can also extend to other partnerships I form related to real estate.

AD: This sounds a little like the Father, Son and Holy Ghost to me, if you will forgive my Catholic Church background. Isn't this confusing to others?

JV: Not in the least for the following reasons. Although Rick appointed me President, that is a title that I very seldom employ. Although I am constantly committed to our company growth, this is much more of Rick's domain, with me devoting virtually all of my time to Vanderblue Associates and my Vanderblue Team. As anyone who knows me would attest, I never introduce myself to anyone as the president of anything, and instead merely Julie. Therefore, these titles are much more resume relevant than every day announcements.

AD: How much of your focus is on the company, versus the associates, versus your team?

JV: Great question. The overwhelming percentage of my time is devoted to the development and needs of the members of The Vanderblue Team and the servicing of all our clients, including mine.

AD: What is the difference between The Vanderblue Team and Vanderblue Associates?

JV: Vanderblue Associates is the umbrella that both The Vanderblue Team and other small and independent teams work under.

AD: Why wouldn't you just have these smaller teams fold into The Vanderblue Team?

JV: Because they are led by a team leader who wishes to grow their personal and individual team brand and are usually further geographically than my core team members. However, they want to benefit through association with the Vanderblue brand and all of the marketing, training, and support services associated with Vanderblue.

AD: Since you acknowledge that the majority of your focus is on The Vanderblue Team itself, let's now turn to how The Vanderblue Team came about, starting with you, Julie. What is your background, how long have you been in the business, and why did you enter real estate?

JV: My background includes personal and professional time both in and out of Connecticut, but the majority of my life has been right here in my great home state. I graduated from the University of Connecticut with a degree in marketing. During college I ran a number of small college related businesses. After college I worked in California and Colorado, both in advertising as well as starting my own business called Julie's Java, which ended up as five small coffee shops throughout ski country.

AD: You mean you were Starbucks before they existed.

JV: I wish. But it was a great experience and satisfied my entrepreneurial cravings.

AD: Why did you move back to Connecticut?

JV: I missed my family and Connecticut. At that time, I was working in advertising design and helping small businesses create marketing strategies including branding, text, and placement.

AD: How did you switch to real estate?

JV: Well, the best part of moving back to Connecticut was meeting and then marrying Thor Vanderblue. By the way, my maiden name was Julie Trotta. Thor was and is a high quality luxury builder. After seeing the way that realtors were marketing his and other properties, and especially given my degree and experience in marketing, I decided this was an opportunity for me to leverage my background.

AD: How many years ago was this?

JV: Approximately 20.

AD: How did you take to your new field?

JV: Since the town of Fairfield is located on the Long Island Sound can I say, like a fish to water? Seriously though, although my motivation initially was to just market my husband's properties more professionally, within a short period of time I was the leader in sales in the town of Fairfield.

AD: Which company did you work for?

JV: My first company was Coldwell Banker, and then I was recruited to join a team at the Ravies Company. It is a great company, highly respected, and Bill Ravies, deservedly so, is a legend in our business. This team was and continues to be highly successful as well.

AD: I agree with everything that you said, and I especially agree with the respect which Bill Ravies commands throughout the entire industry. So two questions: why did you join a team and also why did you leave Ravies?

JV: I wanted to join a team because my husband and I had the first two of our three children at the time, and I wanted to take advantage of how teams can cooperate regarding the demands on one's time. I have always, going back to childhood and university, been a big believer of teams, whether I lead them or helped to comprise them. The reason I left was that I was philosophically at odds with that team's culture.

AD: How do you mean?

JV: My vision of a team was that it would involve specialization, high collaboration, and esprit de corps. And this team was highly individualized, detached, and competitive amongst team members. Do not get me wrong, this team was and is very professional and has attracted very high quality producers. It was just a clash over the culture with me personally.

AD: Why not then just stay in the company and start your own team?

JV: That is precisely what I did. I started my own team, and as a byproduct of my team doing well, I quickly became the number one agent and the overall office number one at headquarters in probably eight to ten months.

AD: How long did it take you to become the number one in Fairfield for Ravies?

JV: Approximately three and a half years.

AD: Who was the first person you hired after you started your first team at Ravies?

JV: It was my first administrator who worked for me on a part time basis. The next person I hired was my first buyer's agent. I hired these two individuals based upon the adage that necessity is the mother of invention. I concluded that there was no way I could handle all of my business either administratively or with the time required to work with buyers based upon the level of business that my marketing and networking were creating.

AD: It seems as though your background as a marketing executive and your natural networking skills were far in advance of either your administrative or time management skills.

JV: Exactly. These first two hires built a foundation for what would grow during my Ravies years to a team of eight people doing well in excess of $120 million in production.

AD: Why did you leave a highly respected company led by an industry giant, given that your team was producing over $100 million?

JV: Because back then I found that my vision and the culture I wanted to create involved conflict with the vision of the company.

AD: How so?

JV: Bill did not support my idea to highlight the individual success of team members. I wanted their names on sign riders and wanted to change my team name from Julie Vanderblue to The Vanderblue Team in order to create greater focus on the team as the brand. This was not acceptable to Bill back then. Today, I do not think it would be a problem there. In fact, I commend Bill for changing his brand emphasis from The Bill Ravies Company to just Ravies.

AD: Well, as a local legend in Fairfield County and having developed a most impressive team, you could have moved anywhere. Why The Higgins Group?

JV: In two words - Rick Higgins. I felt when I met him that Rick was the most humanistic, collaborative, gentle, and caring person I had ever met in real estate. Over the past 14 or so years, this feeling I had has only grown into an absolute fact. Beyond these personal qualities, Rick is an Ivy League graduate, former attorney, and a builder. What a background! Rick convinced me then, and he still convinces me today, that he will do everything to support both individuals and teams. And he does.

AD: How big is The Higgins Group?

JV: We have 14 offices in southeastern Connecticut, but principally in magnificent Fairfield County with offices from Greenwich through Bridgeport.

AD: When you made the transition how many of your team members moved over with you?

JV: All but one.

AD: Let's now move more to the present. How many people are on your team now and how much business are you doing?

JV: Beyond my administrative and marketing support, which consists of three full time people, The Vanderblue Team consists of a core group of ten full time professionals. Regarding production let me first say that we are coming out of several years of a market downturn. In spite of this, we have consistently produced in the $125 million range. But this year we have doubled our team to 20, and I project that we will do approximately $200 million over the next 12 months.

AD: How do you go about selecting the right people for your team?

JV: There are four factors I weigh:

1. Do they predict a capacity for team work and overall collaboration? For this I look for a background of sports or group participation.
2. Can they bring a specialized skill or interest? For example, although I encourage all team members to also be listing and selling generalists, I look for specialties such as first time buyers, investment properties, horse properties, luxury marketing, distressed properties, etc. This way the sum of all of our parts also defines our team in a way reminiscent of a medical group.
3. Geographical coverage as well as geographical team balance.
4. Candidates who have displayed a propensity for community involvement.

And of course, another important other factor is a background of success with special emphasis on them having an attraction to selling.

AD: How often does your team meet and can you describe what you look to accomplish at these meetings?

JV: We meet religiously each and every Monday morning for the entire morning. At these meetings, I look to have a different team member lead the team meeting. We cover all of last week's activities, market trends, open house traffic, results from the weekend, training issues, as well as possibility thinking and individual and team strategizing. We carefully assess all of our lead generating programs, advertising, and our marketing as well.

AD: Can you give me an example of a distinctive marketing program that you might discuss at your meeting?

JV: A great example is The Vanderblue Team Exclusive Sneak Preview program. This is our highly publicized marketing program which is expressly designed for homeowners who have to sell before they buy, and who wish to test the market by hosting a private showing to highly prepared buyers and key rainmaking realtors. This enables our clients to make the necessary staging and pricing adjustments, not just based on the suggestions of one of our team members, but instead we provide real time and more expansive intelligence regarding their property's appeal relative to price.

We have to take the time to review and train our people in a program like this. Does this sneak preview program limit competition and exposure, and therefore hurt our sellers? What we have learned and what we teach is two-fold. First of all, we need to be completely transparent, have a waiver of cooperation form signed, explain how we will initially be trading off full and general competition for a brief period of smaller but more intense competition, and make sure all pros and cons are discussed. Second, this program must also invite and include other companies and their agents, as long as they know that there will be a sneak preview period prior to going to full market.

Because we are in a Manhattan related marketplace and since the Manhattan real estate community has leveraged this concept for decades, our sophisticated clients love having this option.

AD: As a full marketing exposure individual, I must say I respect how you position this option to your clients.

JV: It's amazing how buyers act differently when they know they have a onetime chance. Typically, our properties go very shortly to full market, but our clients who need to sell fast, yet at a strong price, or who want some test marketing first, love this program.

AD: How much of your marketing and technology is Vanderblue generated versus Higgins?

JV: Almost all of it. I pay for Zillow, Trulia, Realtor.com, Top Producer, and encourage team members to invest more into their careers on top of this.

AD: What makes your team distinctive from other teams?

JV: Two words again: Marketing and Community

AD: Give me some examples.

JV: When it comes to community participation, charity work, community educational seminars, event marketing, and merchant partnerships, I have never seen any company of our size as prolific as we are in this area. I could fill a book myself on these programs and efforts. In fact, if any of Debbie's and your readers wants to learn of all we do they can email me.

AD: What is this merchant partnering you've just mentioned?

JV: Most of my Vanderblue Team local advertising, brand building, and personal promotion are completely subsidized by strategic merchant partners. I would also be happy to share copies of these ads and marketing pieces.

AD: I see on your website you refer to AIRE. Please explain what this is.

JV: AIRE stands for All Inclusive Real Estate. Given my marketing background, I always pay close attention to what consumers are asking for, and as all team leaders know, both buyers and sellers are always asking me and my Vanderblue team members to recommend real estate and lifestyle related merchants and professionals.

AD: You mean full service, one stop shopping real estate.

JV: No, not in the hackneyed, limited, and stereotypical way in which some in our industry have confused this.

AD: What do you mean confused?

JV: It's simple. Some real estate companies asked themselves, "What can we sell that will make us the most amount of money? We will call that one stop shopping or full service." Specifically, they would start their own mortgage and escrow company, and this profiteering opportunity meant, to them, one stop shopping or full service.

AD: And what is wrong with this?

JV: Many real estate agents are uncomfortable steering buyers to their own company's mortgage, title or insurance sector, as they know that often times their company has ownership in these companies.

AD: And how is AIRE different?

JV: One, we do not own any of the dozens and dozens of businesses we recommend. Secondly, full service means extending the service menu to much more than the transaction. Our team wants to endorse merchants and professionals who we carefully vet both before, during, and long after the transaction.

In exchange for being a trusted advisor, one willing to share the knowledge of our entire team regarding the best merchants, vendors, and professionals, we generate good will and referrals from both consumers and our AIRE dream team of service providers. I invite your readers to go to our team website: http://www.vanderblue.com/about-our-team/

AD: You also mention community. Elaborate please.

JV: Every town and city in our market is distinctive, and homeowners appreciate how our Vanderblue Team has created world class videos that deliver the most powerful reasons to move to that town or community. On our site we have links to videos on each of these towns and town specific websites, whereby local homeowners and residents in general can post reviews.

AD: Julie, how do you train your team?

JV: We include training in our Monday morning meetings. I am constantly training my team on how to make a Vanderblue Team related marketing presentation to homeowners and I am constantly training team members in the field. This is all in addition to the very effective training Rick Higgins provides all Higgins agents and teams.

AD: How do you find the time for all of this? As I understand, you also occasionally teach at Bridgeport University.

JV: I have a great team that cares about me, as I care about each of them. Because of this I am able to take vacations to Norway each year, the homeland of my husband Thor, and a number of other precious family vacations. Plus, when you love your business, your team, your company, your industry, your community and most of all, your family, you never complain about how hard you work. And I never do.

AD: Well given the demands of your time, on behalf of Debbie and myself, thank you for contributing to *Building Bigger, Busier, and More Profitable Teams.*

The Power of Praise and How It Impacts the Productivity of Teams

By: Debbie De Grote

Most reading this book have heard the following expression on numerous occasions: Nobody cares how much you know, until they first know how much you care.

You may think that this is an odd subject to discuss in a book on teams and yet, as a coach to many, many top teams I can share with you that a lack of praise and appreciation for their members have caused many team leaders to lose outstanding talent. In fact, some team leaders are so harsh and brittle that they have their team members scrambling to please them, stressed out and burnt out, and the turnover of staff and agents on the team is like a parade of candidates coming in the front door and leaving quickly out the back. The team leaders who do not embrace the concept of praising their teams are often themselves burnt out, since they are consumed with hiring and training new talent as they can't keep the talent they have.

I mentioned in the first chapter that one thing all of our interviewees had in common is a passion for what they do. I hope you will notice another common thread that runs through the interviews is their appreciation for their team members and the broker that stands behind them.

One team leader I spoke to today said, "They are the wind beneath my wings and I would not be the dominant market presence I am without them," and he said he tells them this every day.

I wanted to be sure that this book was not solely devoted to the strategic, tactical, and high tech excellence surrounding building bigger, busier, and more profitable real estate teams and groups while completely ignoring the team members themselves. People need praise and collaboration to thrive.

I read once a quote that has stuck with me, "Innovation does not occur in a dictatorship."

Whether you are a team leader, manager, or broker remember the power of praise and collaboration. People will often do more for recognition than they will do for money.

When Walt Disney was expanding Disneyland he would often pull a janitor, a ticket taker, and the girl in the snow white costume into a conference room and ask them for their opinion on a new attraction he had on the drawing board. He would, in essence, attempt to extract someone from all positions in the park.

Disney's employees loved him; they felt valued and retention of staff was outstanding.

When each team member feels valuable they are more likely to contribute at a higher level to team production and more likely to go the extra mile for their customers. Why? Because they feel part of something special, because they are proud of their team and the service it provides.

There is a quote I often hear, perhaps you too are familiar with it. "It is amazing what people can accomplish when no one cares who gets the credit." With all due respect to the original author of this quote, my thinking has always been along the lines of, "It's amazing how much can be accomplished when we give people proper credit for what they individually achieve."

People crave individual praise, not group or company praise. Without question there is an unmistakable correlation between retention and praise!

For all you team leaders, I understand that many of you, like I am, are a high **D** personality and that praise and building camaraderie may not be your go to. (More on this in our chapter entitled, "Talent Examined." You can also go to Excelleum.com and find the link to take your DISC assessment under Free Resources. Have your entire team take it too… it's free!)

High **D** people are action-focused first and foremost, and sometimes tend to forget to focus on the people. Banter, laughter, and singing the praises of my team are not top of mind for me either, so what do I do? I write myself notes, I put it in my calendar, and I work hard to remind myself to curb my directness and to be reasonable in my demands for perfection.

Tips for team leaders on how to praise your team members:

1) Pay attention to their accomplishments, both personal and business.

2) Recognize the situations in which they go the extra mile for a team member or a client.
3) Consider setting aside the first five minutes of every team meeting to praise and acknowledge those who deserve it. When giving recognition be specific and sincere.
4) Consider sharing glowing client testimonials with the entire team.
5) Allow team members to rotate as the team meeting leader.
6) Ask for input. Let them know their ideas and suggestions may not always be something you will act on, however you are always willing to listen with an open mind.
7) Try your best not to interrupt or belittle their contributions, be patient and hear them out.
8) Set a monthly team goal with a bonus end of month celebration if the team achieves the goal.
9) Don't just praise results, praise efforts. Remember, people cannot always control the results but they can always control the effort.
10) Encourage the team to find ways to be of service to the community and praise them for doing so.
11) Praise them in public but criticize them in private, and when you do criticize remember to criticize only the behavior, not the person.
12) Remember and celebrate their birthdays and other milestones in their life. This shows them they are a person to you that matters and not merely a commodity.
13) Send a letter of recognition/congratulations to the agents spouse or significant other.

Give them a little attention and praise, and watch them bloom!

Self-Praise and Public Promotion

As Allan Dalton and I collaborated on this book, he brought something to my attention. Teams really need to pay special attention to how they self-praise and promote themselves to the consumers in their community.

He compared real estate teams and groups to medical or legal groups where collaborative teams and partnerships have thrived for decades.

If we take a close look specifically at how law firms promote themselves, you will see that their ads and website biographical information is much more sophisticated and compelling than most top teams.

I concluded that is for two major reasons:

1) They focused on their skills instead of their service.
2) They focused on their attributes versus their results.

First, we will focus on skills versus service. While both are clearly important, out of the 100 ads I read in *Best Attorney Advertising*, each with two paragraphs explaining their value, I did not find the word service even used once.

Why is this? Can you even imagine 100 real estate agents or companies writing two paragraphs and not including service? Most likely not.

Here is why:

Lawyers want to charge high fees, and high fees seem more justifiable when paying someone from the skill sector as opposed to the service sector.

To lawyers, skills equal fees. Service equals tips.

There are a few reasons why small groups of attorneys and doctors advertise their qualities more than results. First of all, people know most statistics are questionable and showing them can appear boastful. Also, the truth of the matter is that not every law or medical group enjoys the best stats.

Let's take a look at just a few of some of the hundreds of ads I read, ads written by attorney groups and their marketing teams.

"What impressed us even more than the many accolades your firm has received was the humaneness with which you treated us." (Remember, social proof or testimonials are one of the best forms of advertising and persuading.)

"Our firm is proud of what we do and even prouder of the people we represent."

"We have an incredible support staff who is intimately involved with our clients to ensure they receive exceptional professional support."

"Improving a client's quality of life is our firm's number one priority."

"We take on and thrive with the toughest cases."

"There is nobody, absolutely nobody, who will beat us for lack of diligence. We will not be out fought or out thought."

Now by way of contrast, let's take a look at the way teams often self-praise and promote themselves.

"We are spouses selling houses."

"List with us and start packing."

"(name of agent), a houseSOLD name."

"When only the best will do!"

"Dedicated to exceptional service."

"100% committed to helping you achieve your dreams."

"We are number one."

"We are the HOME team."

I could go on and on, however I think you get it. You need to carefully consider your self-praise and promotion if you want to increase your value in the eyes of your customers and clients, as well as your professional presence in your community.

Praising Your Broker

Okay, we have talked about praising your team and praising and promoting your team to the community, now it's time to talk about how to praise your broker.

Your praise and appreciation needs to extend to your company, your broker, and your brand.

Please take note of how Mike McCann and Julie Vanderblue sing the praises of their broker owners. Also how many others in the book, such as the Stanfield Group, give praise and show respect to their brand. This type of praise and respect is not only appropriate, it is good business.

When teams and their team leader criticize the broker they create an unpleasant environment for their people and they can become a negative force in the company.

On the other hand, teams who acknowledge and appreciate the support and resources the brokerage and the brand provides, often find that the broker will then go out of their way to be helpful and supportive of the team's growth.

How top teams show respect for their brokers:

A. They consistently show respect to the company in front of their team.
B. They are able to achieve a win-win compensation arrangement.
C. They encourage the team members to support the company recommended affiliates, who in a sense become extended members of their team.
D. They teach the team members to respect and be grateful to the corporate staff of the brokerage.
E. They teach the team members to follow company protocol and procedures.
F. They set a high standard of excellence and integrity that resonates through the entire company and even throughout the local market.
G. The team leader supports at least some of the company functions and meetings, encouraging the team to attend them all.
H. They praise the broker publicly, look for ways to help the broker recruit by giving their endorsement in writing and verbally when they can, and participate occasionally in events, panels, and sessions designed to help the broker retain existing agents or recruit veterans.

By doing these, the team leader is not only showing respect, he or she is also showing gratitude by giving back to the company.

Brokers Need to Praise Their Teams

Over the years I have heard stories from top producing team leaders about how their brokers disrespected them and made them feel almost as if they were a burden to the company rather than an asset. I do, of course, realize that some teams can be a negative drain on the company resources and disruptive to the culture. If that is the case, then the broker should and must do all that they can to remedy the problem. I suspect that sometimes the brokers or managers are overwhelmed or intimidated by their mega teams and simply do not know how to manage them.

If you are a broker and have powerful and productive teams in your company, don't take them for granted. Praise them in front of their team members when you can, as it helps them retain their talent. And if you, like many of the brokers we coach, need guidance on how to work better with them, then reach out to me and I will connect you with one of my senior team coaches.

Offer guidance, advice, and encouragement. Real estate is a draining and taxing business and even the most successful rock stars need cheerleaders.

Praise them whenever possible in the real estate community. For example, write press releases about their accomplishments that they can use in their marketing. Make them feel welcome and valued, as your endorsement enhances their credibility in the eyes of the consumer.

If you have chosen, as a broker, to be a team-centric company, your rewards for supporting and praising your existing teams will be that you will become known in your market as the place to be if you are a top producing team.

I hope this chapter on praise will be something you read again and again because if you decide that praise matters, it will impact your team culture in many positive ways. It might interest you to know that science reveals that praise releases dopamine, a neurotransmitter that influences the reward center of the brain. And you know as well as I do, rewards lead to confidence and confidence leads to greater individual and team results.

As I conclude this chapter let me praise you for taking the time to read it. I thought I would leave you with a few quotes regarding praise that might inspire you!

It is a great sign of mediocrity to praise moderately.
Luc de Clapiers

The only praise I would like and treasure is the promotion of the activities to which my life is dedicated.
Gandhi

All cruel people describe themselves as paragons of frankness.
Tennessee Williams

Straightforwardness without invitation is rudeness.
Unknown

From Team Leader to Brand CEO

An interview with Gino Blefari

Allan Dalton: Gino, the reason why Debbie De Grote and I are thrilled that you are being interviewed for this book is not only because of your present position as CEO of HSF Affiliates, which operates the brands Berkshire Hathaway HomeServices, Real Living Real Estate, and Prudential Real Estate but also because of the many years you devoted to being an exceptional real estate team leader. Therefore, let's begin with when and why you entered the real estate business.

Gino Blefari: The way I entered the real estate business was actually by accident. It wasn't strategic at all. I put myself through college by working at the Cherry Chase Golf and Country Club in Sunnyvale, California. After graduating from college, a developer bought the golf course and I was given the title of Director of Golf. In this position, I was golf course superintendent, pro shop manager, bar and restaurant manager ... I was even the swim team coach! Along with the job, I was given a residence on the golf course. Pretty good deal for a 23 year old, wouldn't you say?

AD: Indeed! So tell me, how did that go?

GB: It went very well. You know Allan, I've always said the real estate business is not for the weak-willed or faint of heart; it's for those of us who get sick to our stomach if we're not in the top 10 percent of any competitive activity. Along those lines, I wanted to know the record number of rounds per year that had ever been sold before at the golf course. The first year I was in charge of the entire operation, we broke that 26 year record of 25,000 rounds of golf sold by selling 26,000. The next year we sold 42,000 rounds of golf, and the third year we sold an amazing 58,000 rounds of golf. All of these results were from what I learned at the San Jose State School of Business. For example, one of my professors, Dr. Pete Zidnak, had recommended a book I had never heard of before. The book was Dale Carnegie's iconic *How to Win Friends and Influence People*. However, Allan, I knew that my time to win friends and influence people was about to change. That was because all the fun and work I enjoyed at the golf course came to an abrupt end when the developer decided to close down the golf course and build homes on the expensive golf course land. Because of my reputation for hard work and results, I was offered a construction job as the homes were being built.

And though I love to work hard, cleaning the houses and sites was very unfulfilling, even though the pay was pretty good.

AD: So when did real estate come into the picture?

GB: Well, everything changed one day when a brand new BMW pulled up to our site and a well-dressed young man stepped out. I instantly identified with his persona, and so I asked around about him and found out that he sold real estate. Well, Allan, if a picture's worth a thousand words, the picture he portrayed, one of fun and success, instantly made me sign up for a real estate course at the College of San Mateo. And that's how I got into real estate.

AD: I wonder if that real estate salesperson, instead of driving up in an elegant suit and luxury automobile, instead drove up in a buy-a-wreck car and was disheveled, would that mean that the real estate industry might have been deprived of one Gino Blefari?

GB: No, the industry would not have been deprived, but I would have been. One thing I also learned was the power of the first impression. We should all be mindful as salespeople, managers, executives and overall leaders of how important the first impression truly is. In other words, if I wasn't impressed by him I would've had no interest in joining the real estate industry.

AD: Gino, in keeping with the importance of the first impression, I want to use the example of how you introduced a dress code for all those who were part of your real estate team as my segue into your days as a real estate team leader. Specifically, I want to talk to you about the years when you ran your office as a complete and unified team.

GB: Great. The development, growth, and leadership of real estate teams and groups has always been one of my favorite subjects.

AD: What did the beginning of your real estate career look like?

GB: I took my first job with the brokerage firm Fox & Carskadon in the mid-80s. In 1988, I joined Contempo Realty. Here's what I knew: there were a lot of people who knew more about real estate than I did, but I also knew that no one, let me repeat, *no one*, would ever out-work me, out-study me, or out-prepare me.

AD: What is the difference between an office manager and a real estate team leader?

GB: It seems as though today, within most large real estate brokerages, there are multiple leaders. For example, one of the leaders of a real estate office consisting of between 50 and 200 agents is the office manager. Then you often have one or more team leaders within the same office. This begs the question: Is it possible to have only one leader, the office manager? Can one leader convert the entire real estate office into one cohesive real estate team? An office now converted to a team where every associate is dedicated to the same real estate goals and all are rowing in the same direction? This is precisely what I did in my office. I studied team dynamics for years within the corporate world, sports and symphonies. I was determined to discover whether this structure of teams could function in a conventional real estate environment.

AD: Were you able to accomplish this?

GB: With what I experienced and what I was able to develop, yes. But it meant that every person in the office had to commit to team principles or they could not work there. And I believe this structure would probably work best in an office of less than 30 agents.

AD: Gino, you make me want to apologize for my real estate brokerage career. Some top producers believe they can individually make more money outside of a team, and some feel they can make more within a team. Some real estate team leaders believe they can do better managing a smaller team than leading an entire real estate office. That said, when you can be the number one producing agent, have one of the most productive offices in the country, generate significant profits for the company, of which you became an owner, your particular system is worthy of being in the mix. Now tell us, how have you accomplished all of this? And, why did you want to leave being the number one producing agent for managing an office?

GB: First of all, I would not have joined the Contempo management team unless I could still list and sell as that was how Contempo was set up because at the time when I started the offices were very small and all managers sold.

AD: Why was this so important to you, besides the obvious that you were one of the highest-earning agents in America?

GB: Because representing buyers and sellers, and making a monumental impact on the lives of individuals and families, was in my blood. After all, in 1991 as an office manager and team leader, I still personally sold 71 homes in one of America's highest-priced markets. This was during a recession. In fact, I watched many agents leave the business and I actually prospected them for referrals. What I found out was they weren't doing enough business to sustain themselves; however, they were a good source of two to five referrals. I told them that I did not want to abandon home sellers when they needed us most. I also wanted to help buyers who now, for the first time, could buy a home at an affordable price and therefore accomplish their American Dream. I loved the business of helping consumers so much that I started teaching a real estate course at a local community college in order to spread the word about real estate careers to young students.

AD: Tell me about your dress code and the other rules and regulations you implemented while running your team.

GB: First of all, the original office was 95% male and the average age of an agent was 26 years old. Because we were so young, I was concerned that we would not be taken seriously for a buyer or a seller making what would be typically the largest investment of their lives. So I wanted my team to look as conservative as possible and I required them all to wear a tie. I also felt that a white shirt was the most conservative color and if anyone set a foot in the office without a tie on that person was fined $5. To offset that they would get $1 credit for every day that agent wore a white shirt. The money was collected very much like a sports team would do in a kangaroo court.

AD: Well, give me some numbers, so we can see how your no-nonsense, team-centric, all-in approach to managing an office actually worked.

GB: Here's an interesting thing: In 1989 I had 23 agents in my office/team. Everyone called it "Gino's Guys" not Gino's team. Of those 23 agents, and again, this is in 1989, 17 earned over $100,000 a year.

AD: Impressive, as that would probably be like $300,000 a year or so today.

GB: No, Allan. If you actually think about it, the average sales price, conservatively speaking, is five times what it is today. So, it would be like having an office of 23 agents where 17 of them earned over $500,000 a year.

AD: Do you have another example for us regarding how you ran the office at Contempo?

GB: I showed up every day at a coffee shop at 6:30 a.m. with the members of my team working on my personal deals and met several of the other teammates at the office at 7 a.m. to do some type of education, which also would include role-playing.

AD: You actually had your team meetings at 7 o'clock in the morning?

GB: Yes, and weekly we had an office meeting that started at 8:30 a.m. At our 8:30 meeting, we would have 100% attendance and everyone would show up on time.

AD: I think you are wise to concede that each broker needs to decide the way in which their entire company functions, just as you did, first at Contempo and then at your iconic Intero Real Estate Services.

GB: If a structure is created that helps the consumer, agents, teams, the office and the company, and this is all created with the proper proportionality, then and only then will certain brokers sign off on it. In fact, if a team and a brokerage are not set up as a win-win, I will discourage brokers from supporting teams. That said, one must completely respect these exceptionally talented and honorable team leaders who represent an enormous benefit to their brokerages. The challenge is to arrive at what is best and fair all around. This must be decided by broker/owners in conjunction with their team leaders.

AD: Well, said Gino. How else do you set yourself apart?

GB: Well, hundreds of thousands of real estate professionals will state that they are in business for themselves but hesitate to invest in their only true asset - themselves. One of my biggest personal investments is reading thousands of books. In fact, a day does not pass where I do not listen to some type of book. I have always liked the expression that when you are through changing, you are through.

AD: Knowledge is one thing and execution by one's team members is something completely different, although they need to go hand in hand. So, what was your method of ensuring that your team members would execute?

GB: That would be my four disciplines of execution. I refer to this as my West Coast Offense. Here they are:

> Discipline 1 is the discipline of focus. We call this WIG - widely important goals. If your team members have too many goals

they wind up accomplishing no goals. We want vertical, deep focus on a few goals versus horizontal and thin focus on numerous goals.

Disciple 2 is the discipline of leverage. Act on your lead measure. A lead measure is different than a lag measure. Lag measures deal with the past, and thus it is too late. Lead measures deal with trajectory and trending, predictive data.

Discipline 3 is the discipline of score-keeping. Have a compelling scoreboard. As in sports, where you can observe the intensity and focus exponentially increasing when the scores go up on the scoreboard, so too this occurs when we memorialize results in business by making them unavoidably visible and on a scoreboard. We focus on lag and lead measures, just as a sporting event, except the game is never over.

Discipline 4 is the discipline of accountability. Creating a cadence of accountability. For example, I would have a team call twice a week, one on Monday and the other on Friday. The purpose of the call, which I called our WIG call, was for team members to announce their lead measure. An example of this would be, "I committed to making 25 phone contacts, I made 26. I committed to knocking on 100 doors. I knocked on 105 doors. I committed to pop by five past clients. I popped by six. Next week I am committing to make X number of phone contacts, knocking on X number of doors and popping by X number of clients." All I would do is listen and keep score. That is the cadence of accountability.

AD: This sounds like a great system for any sales organization. Gino, thank you for sharing your amazing wisdom with our readers.

A Broker in the Business to Build Teams

An interview with Rick Dubord

Debbie De Grote: Rick, the reason why I am so excited to have you participate in our book about real estate teams is because you don't have a team, but instead you are a broker who is completely dedicated to building a real estate company throughout British Columbia comprised essentially of real estate teams.

Rick Dubord: You are absolutely correct Debbie.

DD: What is the name of your firm?

RD: HomeLife Benchmark Realty.

DD: Rick, when did the light bulb go off for you that developing a real estate team culture was the way for HomeLife Benchmark Realty to go?

RD: Well Debbie, we had a presence in the marketplace with some of our teams. But nothing of the magnitude of what I encountered when I heard Ben Kinney, while at an Inman Conference, speak of his team in Bellingham, Washington doing in excess of 600 transactions and how the team was organized and run.

DD: So it sounds as though this experience led you to want to go all in for teams.

RD: It did.

DD: What actions did you begin to take to promote the team concept in your market?

RD: One thing I did was at the board level. Because I am on the Broker Council, I ensured that at the board they became more sensitive and understanding of teams. Specifically, in that they needed to extend their recognition policies to include team acknowledgement. For HomeLife I researched what successful teams were doing, and therefore what we could do from a company support position to encourage teams and help them to flourish. We also, with your help Debbie, and through the Excelleum DISC program, developed a multi-level interviewing process geared to determining team suitability for prospective team members. Therefore, through our online and then offline interviewing, aided by our behavioral analysis program, we could now help guide them to the best team match for them within the company. I decided that unlike how some brokers either resist or tolerate teams that I wanted to be seen, because I believe I am, as the most dedicated to all that real estate teams represent of anyone, if not in the entire industry, at least in Canada.

DD: And when was this particular eye opening Inman Conference which you attended?

RD: About three years ago. Yet this past year it seemed as though 50% of the conference was devoted to real estate teams. In some cases there were teams who had more support staff than buyer agents. I experienced teams there who had PR departments and social media directors. These teams seemed to be better organized than most of the brokers, and certainly more strategic.

DD: From this exposure, what did you consider to be the most valuable service you could provide your company teams?

RD: After I interviewed all of our teams it became clear that their greatest deficiency, void, or need was in the preparing of their team financials. They essentially were challenged in what true financials were. Therefore, I am now in the process of developing a system, through the software I have acquired, that can provide our teams with their financials each month. Because we already have all of their transactions recorded, all I will need is for them to post their expenses and a few other items in order to have this confidential report sent exclusively to the team leader.

DD: That is remarkable Rick. Is there anything else you wish to provide as a team resource to all of HomeLife teams?

RD: That would be appointment setting for buyer agents who wish to schedule showings for team member properties.

DD: That is fantastic Rick.

RD: Debbie, anything that we can do to make team efficiencies scale across all of our teams means a win-win for our teams and, therefore, our company.

DD: Rick, it sounds to me that while most brokers want real estate teams to fit in with the company, you are actually determined that your company fits in with your teams.

RD: That is a brilliant observation. What you just said completely encapsulates everything I am determined to do for our teams.

DD: It sounds as though you have taken all of your business acumen, and now industry knowledge, to set up a Real Estate Teams Concierge Service.

RD: Debbie, you completely get what we are doing, I love that description too!

DD: Since this book is titled *Building Bigger, Busier, and More Profitable Teams*, where do you see this real estate team movement heading?

RD: Well, in our Clovervale office 60% of our production is done by teams. This trend will only continue to increase, as I have tracked it and it has increased each of the last two years. Individuals are increasingly learning that they are losing business strictly due to their not being on a team. This is because teams are preparing members on how to be successful better than the company at large. It is simple. Someone on a team can explain to a home seller that they provide both everything the company has to offer as well as the team, so it's sort of a no brainer.

DD: Are you seeing that the more quality person who comes to interview with the company now wants to be with a team?

RD: When given the choice, almost always they want to join one of our teams. And our teams can document countless examples of agents who were with our company for years who, upon joining a team, witnessed significant productivity increases. They recognize the benefit of being under the care of a current rainmaker. They are willing to receive less commission to make a lot more money due to doing much more business.

DD: Other than the compensation plan that the company has for all agents, do you try to influence how each team compensates their agents?

RD: No, I leave this completely to each team leader. There must be a certain degree of sameness here, but they also all compete among one another for team members.

DD: If you had your way, would you want everyone to be part of a team?

RD: Well, I do not concern myself with this. It is what it is, it will become what it will become. The market of ideas will decide this. Debbie, I am a futurist so I look at trends and then ride the wave. Traditional brokerage, due to the internet, is not going to sustain itself.

DD: I know through my coaching with HomeLife that you do extensive consumer surveys. When you survey consumers regarding teams and why they choose your people, is it more because of the company brand, the team brand, or a combination?

RD: Almost completely due to the team brand and the respect for individual team leaders.

DD: How prominent is the company brand on your team's marketing?

RD: Usually you will find that we have the minimum of the legal limit.

DD: Rick, you have both office managers and team leaders. What is the value of each and are they synergistic?

RD: Great question Debbie. We still have a large population of agents who do not believe in teams. And our very capable managers and I are also completely committed to their success. We provide superior training, technology, and overall support. Our managers do a great job with this, as well as providing company, industry, and market related info to everyone, including our teams. That said, team collaboration creates a sharing and unity experience unlike anything else I have ever seen in real estate. So at the end of the day, anyone associated with HomeLife can make the career decision, which is influenced by our DISC assessments, as to how they are most likely to perform best. If they want to be on a team, they have team choices. If they want to work outside of a team, they have office choices. It's all quite simple. HomeLife needs to be able to sell everyone that we have the right career path for them. The oldest adage of selling is to first find out what people want and then show them how they can have it. Therefore, we find out what all of our people want and we provide it. In turn, we expect them to do the same with the consumer.

DD: Well thank you Rick, you certainly gave me what I wanted from this interview: honest, riveting, forward thinking, and controversial thoughts.

RD: You are most welcome Debbie, and thank you.

Talent Examined

By Debbie De Grote

Socrates once wrote, "A life unexamined is a life not worth living."

We at Excelleum believe that when it comes to real estate, one's personality traits unexamined can lead to a real estate career not worth living. This is why Excelleum, a coaching and consulting company noted for our customized methods of mentoring, employs the DISC process of determining predictive personal behavior as a staple of our career development programs.

The DISC is an assessment process that reveals which personality traits are more pronounced within all of us. The letters D, I, S, and C serve as an acronym whereby each letter stands for the definitional symbol of each of the four behavioral quadrants. The four symbols are dominance, influence, steadiness, and compliance.

The creation of the DISC goes all the way back to 1928. That was the year that William Marston, for his Harvard University doctoral thesis, wrote the acclaimed "The Emotion of Normal People." His major premise was that four basic personality types, each described by the letters D, I, S, and C, explained virtually all human behavior.

Dr. Marston, however, did not intend that his epic work be utilized for the screening of prospective employees, for career developmental purposes, or for team building guidance. This application came decades later when noted industrial psychiatrist Walter Clarke evolved the DISC for business utilization.

The DISC process is, without question, under-utilized in real estate. I say this, as I believe that while real estate is one of the easiest professions to enter, conversely it is one of the more difficult in which to gain great success. The DISC would significantly help both of these factors.

Given how difficult it is to gain notable success in real estate, I am left proud of both my accomplishments, considering I was making several hundreds of thousands a year in real estate throughout my 20s and 30s, and my many clients who presently enjoy seven figure incomes and benefit from DISC-influenced coaching.

However, there is no doubt in my mind that had I been exposed to the DISC earlier in my career that my income would have been much higher (even though my income then by today's present value would be over one million per year).

I point out the difference the DISC can make after seeing how, as the first step of our customized coaching and consulting, this self-discovery process has transformed numerous careers.

The personality analysis alone is only the beginning. Just as the so-called "Socratic Dialogue" is credited for the deeper understanding of one's self, through conferring and counseling with a trusted mentor, so too the DISC analysis only sets the framework and foundation for the coaching process that follows.

I love the quote attributed to Dr. Rohm, considered by many as the foremost expert of the DISC today, "Strengths can carry you, but your blind spots should concern you."

Speaking of blind spots, it can be said that the real estate industry either has a blind spot, or has largely turned a blind eye towards the individual assessment needs of much of our profession. To some it seems as though our industry is largely indifferent to what the unique qualities and needs of its population might be.

In regards to indifference, I am reminded of what George Bernard Shaw once wrote, "The worst sin towards fellow creatures is not to hate them, but to be indifferent to them. That is the essence of inhumanity."

While collectivized training, office meetings, company meetings, and seminars are geared for one and all, we are an industry crying out for personalized understanding and customized coaching. The DISC immediately suggests the recognition that we are all different and that all of our differences are deserving of understanding and optimization.

My husband Don and I are reminded of the uniqueness of each individual every day of our lives. This is because our precious twin daughters Taylor and Erika, who are each a real estate protégée of Don and myself, each has a distinctive personality as validated by the DISC.

Gino Blefari, CEO of HSF Affiliates and also a career long disciple of coaching and the DISC, is perhaps most convincing in his explanation of what the DISC represents. "As a major believer of the power of storytelling, I look at the DISC as a part of each individual's story, one that we in management should listen to when invited. Moreover, when the DISC process becomes part of your career development culture it automatically symbolizes that you appreciate human distinctiveness and thus do not view people as numbers or interchangeable widgets. Plus the appreciation of diversity begins with the appreciation that each of us is diverse."

Since this chapter is primarily intended to tweak your curiosity about the DISC, rather than to comprehensively explain it (which would be a book by itself), let me now provide what the DISC can mean when properly embraced.

A. Career enhancement takes place when individuals and teams have their assumed strengths validated. This leads to a greater repetition of favorable professional behavior.
B. When counterproductive blind spots are revealed and accepted, this provides the opportunity to amend or eliminate costly behaviors.
C. When one's coach has the privilege of discussing a client's behavioral patterns, it leads to customized solutions and strategies along with shared acceptance of change.
D. The invaluable insights provided through the DISC process enable the coaching process to evolve from symptom related mentoring to cause related coaching.

The DISC, as I said, was not created within the real estate industry and its influence is late in coming. An estimated 50 million people have participated in the DISC program, including wide usage within not only the corporate, government, and military sectors, but also professional sports teams.

My favorite example of how the DISC is so revered outside of real estate is through the example of my own Bob LeFever, one of our Excelleum coaches. Bob, after graduating from Catholic University and before doing graduate work at the University of Virginia, was both taught and in turn taught the DISC method during his years as an FBI agent. Bob, while replete with colorful examples of how the DISC was instrumental in hostage negotiation resolution strategies in the years before enjoying great success as a real estate salesperson and CEO of Coldwell Banker California, is now educating our clients on how to best relate to all other real estate consumers and clients.

Bob is joined by all of his fellow Excelleum coaches and consultants in their adherence to the DISC process. In fact, I have turned down coaches who came to me from other coaching companies because they demonstrated an inability to move away from guru-based, one size fits all coaching.

I have always believed that no two people can sell alike and no two markets or consumers are precisely alike. I learned this firsthand while working with a stunning array of different personalities in my many years of selling in Orange County, California, and I see how different people truly are now that I have my own coaching company.

My Excelleum team and I have also learned that real estate teams and groups are the biggest proponents of the DISC. While real estate companies are supposed to represent a hit or miss opportunity, one where the words recruiting and retention are more celebrated than selection and development, expectations are generally higher that a team will be more selective and more invested in personal development. This nuance makes the DISC all the more relevant to real estate teams and groups.

Real estate teams, by their very nature and definition, suggest more specialization and collaboration. Each of these qualities requires deeper examination of not only specialized skills but also of specialized developmental recognition and assistance. If a real estate team cannot provide superior personal development, then why would someone opt to join a team over becoming a member of the larger brokerage population? Especially when they can boast of greater and less diluted brand clarity to the public.

Most brokers and managers, given the enormous size of many offices and companies today through consolidation, either do not possess the time, the patience, the interest, or the training to be involved in MRI-like examination and mentoring of its individual associates. Therefore, coaching and personal attention is less expected from conventional brokers and managers than from teams.

Real estate teams and groups automatically convey the need for collaboration. This is not anywhere near expected in the general brokerage population. Therefore, these much smaller groups of team members increasingly expect more specialized and personalized attention and understanding. This is where the DISC uniquely helps teams. We find that most real estate team leaders are more accomplished at being a listing rainmaker, a local well branded real estate celebrity possessing the ability to deliver rousing messages to the team, but too busy to become dedicated to the necessary disciplines involved in the sustainable career development coaching that the DISC program influences.

Conflict resolution is another key aspect. The DISC is often more important for teams due to how their smaller number of individuals all presumably working as a team (versus for an office or company) can find a conflict much more disruptive.

The purpose of this chapter, as stated, is to provide an overview versus a much longer and in depth account of the DISC. If you find yourself wanting that in depth account, we hope that you will contact us.

That being said, let's take a look at how the DISC enables us to better coach our clients regarding prospecting.

Prospecting Techniques and the DISC

Although everyone in real estate is well aware of opportunities such as FSBOs and expired listings, have you ever wondered why such a small percentage of agents truly specialize within these niche markets?

Now without the help of the DISC, your all-encompassing answer may be fear of prospecting. But there is much more, as there is with prospecting reluctance in general.

Let's now examine how behavioral and personality traits play a role in this behavior or avoidance of same.

FSBOs and Expireds:

High **D**

> High Ds will find this as a worthy challenge and will certainly feel up for the task. While you will not need to help them to overcome their fear or hesitancy, where we provide them assistance is with consumer-centric scripting, delicate dialogue, and role play. Given the impulsiveness of Ds, we also need to be prepared for them to have a tendency to quit if not enjoying almost immediate results. We also work with high Ds on moderating their aggressiveness by asking them to explain back to our coaches how everything they say would sound to them if they were the prospect.

High I

They will behave much like the High **D**, but need a little more prompting to make the calls and some coaching role play and reinforcement regarding closing.

High S

They need to be liked, and their sensitivity can actually hurt them. High **S**'s need to be reminded that because they are more people-centric, sensitive, and likeable than the more aggressive and pushy agents, that consumers truly deserve them, even if this means they have to step up their aggressiveness in order to give the homeowners a chance to meet with them.

High C

These are the ready, aim, but don't fire agents. They know they should make these calls, but their heart is not in it. We tend to have them record their calls and listen to them, as well as provide a lot of encouragement. You must set realistic expectations with them, as they are looking for reasons to stop calling since their cautious nature is not consistent with this level of consumer engagement.

Cold Calls:

High D

Just require scripts and encouragement, and you need to help them shed the rough edges that many high **D**s are not aware of (remember blind spots).

High I

Look to make cold calling a community event. Socialize this task with pizzas and camaraderie. Sometimes we look to team them up with fellow associates.

High S

They are typically too reserved and lack the necessary bravado and energy required to inspire consumers spontaneously.

High C

These are task oriented versus people oriented agents, and unfortunately the task of calling is usually drowned out by their lack of people power.

Farming:

High D

While they possess the aggressiveness, many high Ds are checker players and not chess players. Therefore, they need coaching to help them recognize the benefits of strategic planning, reward delay, and organization. We coach them by providing specific examples of how other high Ds have combined instant impact prospecting with systematic delay reward farming.

High I

They enjoy the socialized nature of farming. This provides them with much needed social engagement, but we usually need to help them with messaging proper materials and to evolve from fun loving trinkets to more serious and relevant content.

High S

They will be more inclined to do the antiseptic elements of farming such as marketing materials versus door knocking. We always need to coach them on making sure they are working with high enough volume and message consistency.

High C

They will conceive of what they want to do and organize what they should do, but unless we apply tough love, they simply will not do it.

Sphere of Influence:

We teach our clients that it is not enough to just develop a sphere of influence, but that you also need to influence your sphere.

High D

They understand the importance of building their sphere, but struggle with how to leverage influence. Because they are aggressive, we find it worth our while to constantly work with them on messaging.

High I

They often times excel here more than any other personality type. The social nature of real estate was meant for high Is. Where we coach them is how to convert their social opportunities into business opportunities. This group also takes great pride in their social appearance and reputation.

High S

They need constant reminders of the importance of building and influencing their sphere through specific and targeted campaigns. Since this group is less likely to do cold calling, it is vital that they are all in on sphere of influence and marketing.

High C

The same pattern of excessive preparation and excuses in lieu of activity rears its ugly head here as well. These people require, as in farming and cold calling, strict managing and constant reinforcement, as they are being expected to go against their personality type.

Introducing the DISC to Your Prospective Team Members and Present Team Members

What is the DISC?

The DISC is a personality style assessment that we encourage you to take (or we have you take) in order to help us to determine if you are an appropriate fit for our real estate team.

How does it work?

For several decades the DISC has been helping corporations, governments, the military, and sports teams to identify the strengths and blind spots of each of us. By having access to this unique insight, it enables all of us to better understand how we can maximize our effectiveness either individually or as a part of a working team. It also helps companies and teams like ours become more knowledgeable and sensitive regarding what type of personalities best fit our team's needs.

Does it measure intelligence or aptitude?

Neither. First of all, there are no right or wrong answers. Rather, it measures likelihood of repeated professional behavior.

Will it tell me definitely what personality type I represent?

No, it reflects how all of us are a unique blend of different personality tests but it reveals which one or multiple ones are most disproportionate to others.

Do you hire strictly on the basis of DISC?

Option A:

No, it is just one factor, although a significant one, and it serves as a foundation for more in depth communication with prospective employees. As I said, it is imperfect but considered by many the most predictive of future behavior. That said, many alter their behavior when they become more aware of their personality tendencies, which are a result of both genetics and environment. We are a team that possesses all of these personality types, but we have arrived at some conclusions as to which styles are most suited for particular tasks that our team must manage.

Option B:

What makes our real estate team different in its selection of professional talent is that we believe that we have a sacred responsibility to avoid enabling anyone to end up wasting their precious time and talent by making a career move that is contrary to their self-interest and talents. Therefore, we as a rule do not hire individuals if their personality readings are in conflict with certain team based positions.

How does the DISC arrive at these conclusions?

The DISC includes questions that speak to 15 basic behavioral patterns: Achiever, agent, appraiser, counselor, creative, developer, inspirational, investigator, objective thinker, perfectionist, persuader, practitioner, promoter, respect-oriented, and specialist.

How does it influence team building?

Tomas Premuzik and David Winsborough, in the 2015 *Harvard Business Review* article on DISC and teams, write that the tests reveal which team members are more open minded, and that teams comprised of more open minded members leverage conflict to improve performance, as well as the fact that teams perform better with members who share values. We have learned from our DISC training how to look for these tendencies being present in team candidates.

We are here to help you in the following ways:

A. Help you define your real estate team or group by organizational positions and the suggested personality type for each team role.
B. Help you better identify your professional propensities, either as a team leader, manager, or both.
C. Coach each of your team members as a gift from you for their personal growth, leading to far greater results and profits for your team.
D. Help your team better identify the personality types of the consumers, clients, vendors, fellow agents, and brokers with whom they interact.

Final thoughts:

Dale Carnegie in his book, *How to Win Friends and Influence People*, gave as his eighth principle the following advice: Talk in terms of the other person's interest.

In essence, this is what the DISC is all about.

We at Excelleum would consider it a privilege if you share with us your point of view about your company, your team or you as an individual.

A Mega Team Leader Relying More on Mobile than Brick and Mortar

An interview with Ernie Carswell

Debbie De Grote: Ernie, where, when, and why did you enter the real estate business?

Ernie Carswell: Dallas, Texas, 1985. I entered real estate to feel that I could "chart my own course" and also because it seemed to offer flexible hours.

DD: What did you do before real estate?

EC: Flight attendant, hotel concierge at the Four Seasons, in the buying office for Neiman Marcus as an administrative clerk, residential family therapist at a state mental hospital for troubled youth (during pre-med college years).

DD: How did your prior career pursuits influence what you have done in real estate?

EC: They all deal with the public, sales, and personality issues . . . somehow those challenges still remain!

DD: Talk about your early years. Which company did you begin with and what did you do originally to set your path towards success?

EC: I began with the Henry S. Miller Company, one of the most prominent firms in Dallas during the 1980s, in their Highland Park residential office. My success path was pointed in the direction of watching what the successful agents did, how they lived, and I assumed I would want the same practice and lifestyle. I aligned with other rookie agents and made friendships to talk incessantly about our new business and how to get ahead. We did everything to kick start a career: cold calls, FSBO, door knocking. The most effective results were the relationships gleaned among my peers and a respect between us that helped build trust.

DD: What geographical market did you serve then and now?

EC: I have served three geographical markets: Dallas, New York City, and now Beverly Hills.

DD: What percentage of your business in the early years was from listings versus sales?

EC: The early years was strictly sales, almost no listings.

DD: When did you begin to add service staff to your personal operation?

EC: At about year eight of the business. It began as sharing an assistant (which doesn't work too well) and since my tenth year in the business I have been utilizing full time assistants or administratives consistently.

DD: When did you officially become a team and what name did you select for it? Why?

EC: Officially 1998, called it Carswell Collection, which at the time seemed like a dual term use. The Collection was our property assortment of listings, but also was a collection of professionals working together in an organized fashion.

DD: Who was the first position you hired, why, and what did they do for you?

EC: A full time assistant, their job description was basically, "Help me do everything!"

DD: When you started your team, what company were you with?

EC: Coldwell Banker.

DD: How many other teams were there in the company and was there any resistance to your becoming a team?

EC: Two other teams. We were in the first run of team building. Otherwise, the only "teams" were husband/wife partnerships or parent/child partnerships.

DD: When there is resistance from brokers and company owners, what do you believe causes it?

EC: Brokers tend to think it costs them money somehow. They feel the team leader is taking commission margin that would normally be the company's. Perhaps, but the team leader is running a small company inside the brokerage and handling many managerial and productive responsibilities that lessen the burden on the brokerage. Greed is usually the baseline resistance of brokerages that resist team building, in my opinion.

DD: Getting back to the development of your team Ernie, take me through its growth in terms of personnel including what each function team members serve.

EC: Our team structure is made up of two full time administrative support employees, paid by the team leader, but available for team agent support whenever needed. There are 11 agents (including the team leader) and they are titled Team Partners in brand and on the website/ advertising. The team leader's function is to help promote, teach, and mentor the team partners. There are no buyers' agents who are handed leads exclusively. There is opportunity for a team partner agent to receive a lead from the team leader, but it is earned on productivity, attitude, aptitude, and appropriateness for the client description. It is a fair rationale, but not a rotation basis or roulette wheel type of distributing leads. This is all subjective on the part of the team leader's opinion and direction.

DD: Do you consider yourself more of a team leader or team manager, or both?

EC: Team leader. I would serve as a rather poor manager and try not to manage but to inspire.

DD: Is the function of your team that team members are hired and compensated to support your efforts, or does the team exist to equally support the efforts of all team members...or both?

EC: Teams exists to support each member's efforts to build their career. The team also exists to be a training ground for experienced and for learning agents. It is a frequent occurrence that the team leader will actually learn something from a team partner agent, which is a nice exchange of duties and benefits.

DD: How do you differentiate your team value from the value of the host company?

EC: Team value is intimate and personal. Brokerage value is professional and at arm's length.

DD: How much of your time is devoted to personally working with sellers versus buyers?

EC: 75% sellers / 25% buyers

DD: Do you have team members who both list and sell?

EC: Yes.

DD: Do you assign your team members geographical farms?

EC: No geo farms, we have not found an effective method of carving up LA.

DD: How often does your team meet? Can you describe a typical team meeting?

EC: The team meets once monthly, but more frequently in office environment sittings that are unscheduled but attended by numerous agents. Agents work primarily from home or mobile, so work stations are fluid and not dedicated except for a minimum number of team partners.

DD: What do you do to generate leads and which contact management system do you use?

EC: Word of mouth referrals, returning clients, and occasional cold call leads are our territory. We are not happy with our contact management system, which has been Contactually, so we are taking a break and searching for a more effective base.

DD: What do you think makes your team so successful?

EC: Diversity, experience from previous jobs carried forward to a real estate career, reputation is a major consideration. The team thrives on maintaining the highest ethical standards and we are known for it.

DD: What are some of the distinctive marketing or advertising programs you use?

EC: Social media is becoming more central to our distinctive marketing efforts. We still believe in print advertising, but are very selective when deciding when and where. We use some internet marketing, but are not confident in its effectiveness.

DD: In a sentence or two could you describe your team's culture?

EC: Intellectual, artistic, pursuing best life scenarios in a huge metropolitan area like Los Angeles and creating a sense of "community" and belonging within it.

DD: How much importance do you place on training and coaching for your team members?

EC: For the new recruit, much importance is placed on training, coaching, and mentoring. For experienced agents, all three are still imperative, but at a pace that can be merged with a successful career, and not the absolute requirement that it is for the new recruit agents.

DD: What do you think is the biggest reason agents want to join your team?

EC: Reputation and opportunity for success alignment.

DD: When and if you lose a team member is it more likely they leave, or that they are let go?

EC: More likely they leave of their own free will. Some departures have been financial imperatives because the agent wasn't able to earn a consistent income. Other departures have been emotional in nature when the spirit of alignment slipped out of gear and things began to run off track and in contrast to our normal operating practice.

DD: Do you allow or encourage teams within your overall team?

EC: We have one team within the team and it has worked well for about five years.

DD: How important is it to your team which brokerage or brand you belong to?

EC: It's not as important as the brokerage would normally think, but there are certain brands that we would not consider at all and would not be a good match.

DD: How much volume does your team produce?

EC: $120m in the first 6 months of 2016.

DD: How do you see real estate teams evolving in the future?

EC: As more prevalent and more important.

DD: How has the evolution of real estate teams changed our industry?

EC: It has become commonplace and the natural progression of our industry.

DD: Do real estate teams increase consumer service?

EC: I do believe the team offers a client more service and is more responsive to client needs.

DD: Ernie, do you have plans on selling your team someday, and if so how will you go about that?

EC: I've only recently heard about teams selling themselves as a unit for a price. I haven't fully warmed up to the idea yet, but am observing it with interest.

DD: How big can you see your team growing?

EC: We're big enough, but focus on growing our productivity. That's where we seek growth!

DD: How do you think the internet might change teams in the future regarding growth?

EC: I foresee team "pods" within real estate offices, and those pods will be the center of activity for the team, but only an administrative or team leader will have committed office space on a regular basis.

DD: Thank you Ernie and congratulations on your immense and exemplary success.

From Owning Restaurants to Running a Successful RE/MAX Team

An interview with Martin Clement

Debbie De Grote: Why don't we begin with you telling our readers the name of your company, your team, and how long you have been in the business?

Martin Clement: RE/MAX Core, The Clement Moore Real Estate Group, and 10 years.

DD: What was your background prior to getting into real estate?

MC: I was an entrepreneur and owned three restaurants.

DD: What did you learn from that experience that you have carried forward to your real estate career?

MC: The ability to multitask, to wear different hats.

DD: Why did you start your group?

MC: There were certain real estate tasks that I wasn't thrilled to do anymore, like showing houses and uploading my listings to the MLS. I instead wanted to focus more on where my greater talents and interests lie, specifically lead generation. Plus, I can pay others to handle showings, upload listings, and make appointments for me.

DD: Just as I am sure you didn't do all the cooking, wait on all of the tables, and clean the dishes at the restaurants you owned. How long were you an individual realtor before you started your group?

CM: Interestingly, I started out on a team myself. I began as a buyer's agent. And then after three years I went out on my own.

DD: How would you describe your group's structure?

MC: The size of our team is one listing coordinator, which is administrative, one transaction coordinator, which is also administrative, two listing specialists, and then four buyer specialists.

DD: What percentage of the agents who work for your local RE/MAX broker would you say are on real estate teams?

MC: I would say approximately 25% enjoy team or group affiliation.

DD: It is interesting that you actually came into real estate as a member of a team. While there are other team leaders who also began as a team member, most started outside of a real estate team. What caused you to want to begin as a team member yourself?

MC: I have always believed in the power of specialized knowledge. Specifically, if everyone continues to try to do every task within their business, they will never master any one area. Therefore, it is important to specialize in areas that you either particularly like, or are good at.

DD: So you started out as a buyer specialist. Please share what percentage of your time today is working with buyers.

MC: None. I am 100% a listing specialist.

DD: Walk me through how you made the transition from working with buyers to representing sellers.

MC: At first it is hard to delegate because you think that you, and only you, are best suited to work with the buyers who come to you. Then you realize that someone who only specializes in working with buyers can be far more capable, and that buyers deserve the very best.

DD: When you go on a listing presentation, how do you convey to prospective home sellers how this division of your real estate group benefits them?

MC: We all go through the benefits of specialization and how generalists dilute effectiveness. We bring up comparisons between our team approach versus the acute limitations of only having one agent. That we have four buyer agents at the ready, instantly waiting to move into action any time there is interest directed at their property, or at other properties that will spin off interest for their home.

DD: That is a compelling point, how does it resonate?

MC: Sellers often say, "Why would anyone ever list with just one person instead of a team?"
DD: Do they ever turn your point around and wonder aloud about getting lost in the crowd?

MC: Seldom, because of how specific I am in describing the flawless integration and execution of our team of specialists. But when they do, I remind them that my personal and entire focus is on them and the listing, so if anything, they are much more likely to fall between the cracks when the sole realtor is trying to do too many things.

DD: How do you differentiate your group against other teams in your market?

MC: The RE/MAX difference is second to none. We leverage our local, national, and international immense advantage, as well as the quality of our local RE/MAX network, our great RE/MAX website, and TV advertising.

DD: Why do you think RE/MAX has been so instrumental in the development of real estate teams across the industry?

MC: RE/MAX is very progressive and agent and team centric. On a local level, we have a great local owner and we all learn from him. Whether we are a team or an individual, he helps all of us learn and grow regardless of what our approved business model is.

DD: You are very fortunate.

MC: And so is our entire group.

DD: What would you do if teams were merely tolerated?

MC: Leave. This business is tough enough without having undue stress from within your own company, or with having internal compensation or structural battles. And why would any broker want to turn their back on the most productive agents who take on additional expenses themselves to grow a team? Agents who bring listings, credibility, and results into the local brand.

DD: Why would you not just open your own brokerage?

MC: Because it would not scale for the size of the team I want to lead. My cap is $11,500 with the same for my partner. For each of our team members who is a licensed agent, the cost is $6,000 per year, so we probably pay about $50,000 a year. If I were to open an office, it would probably cost me $35,000 just to have an administrative person at the front desk alone. I would need to find a business location, hire an accountant, and pay for all utilities. Now if I get to the point that I think I would want, or could hire, 150 agents working at my brokerage, then perhaps it would make sense, but not now.

DD: Martin, I appreciate your open and honest revelation that you could not operate on your own, at least right now, as well as you can under the umbrella of your broker/owner. I want to encourage all of our team leaders to reflect on all of the costs their broker/owners have to absorb and be thankful that they have a broker who can build a large enough business for them to operate as they do within its boundaries. So too, I hope that all brokers will recognize how difficult it is for them to hire 100 or so agents without providing top producing, business-minded agents like yourself the opportunity to form teams. At the end of the day, the numbers must work out completely for both sides.

What I love about what you said Martin, is that it honored the business courage of the broker/owner.

MC: You hit it on the head. The numbers must and should work for everybody.

DD: Speaking of numbers, what is your group's volume?

MC: We are presently doing $850,000 in gross commission income, but are looking to do $1 million in group commissions by the end of the year.

DD: You owned three restaurants at one time, what do you presently own?

MC: I own a mortgage company with 10 loan officers. I encourage my loan officers to do business with my agents, and my agents to do business with my loan officers.

DD: How do you leverage the role of your mortgage company when making listing presentations?

MC: We always mention that we own a mortgage company and that we can coordinate the transaction better since both companies are in the same building.

DD: Does having a team have consequences regarding fee validation?

MC: Absolutely. We always point out that they get eight people for the price of one.

DD: Is your group more likely to appeal to top producers or moderate producers who wish to become top producers?

MC: The latter.

DD: How does your group handle lead generation? You mentioned that earlier as your specialty.

MC: We do geo farming, which are neighborhoods of 600 properties. We keep in contact with the neighborhood through our community update system. We also do online lead generation and diverse prospecting.

DD: What do you mean by diverse prospecting?

MC: Targeted marketing on all different types of resale and investment types of properties geared towards different niche markets.

DD: How often does your group meet?

MC: Once a week. We meet every Friday morning at 11. It is mostly about what we need to do to get more listings and get them sold. For example, we review listing inventory overall, absorption rates, how many listings we have, etc.

DD: Why did you choose the name group versus team?

MC: Group sounds more like a collection of equal partners, whereas a team sounds like there is a team leader with too much emphasis on the one person.

DD: Will teams and groups continue to grow at a rapid rate?

MC: Yes. For example, the average agent in our market does seven deals for the whole year. We will do 140 as a group.

DD: What makes your group so effective?

MC: Our obsession with our database and keeping it growing, and our administrative and contact management systems.

DD: What system do you use?

MC: IXACT

DD: Do you sell a lot of your group listings yourself?

MC: Yes, and we offer clients a slight discount also if they have two deals with us simultaneously.

DD: How much of your listing presentation is about RE/MAX?

MC: Put it this way, I have 13 slides and only one is about RE/MAX. Why? Because RE/MAX is so well known and respected you don't have to say much. The rest is about our group, our systems, our results, and me.

DD: Do you share your knowledge with other RE/MAX agents and teams?

MC: All the time. Plus, I also give classes in Montreal.

DD: Is there anything else you would like to share with your fellow team leaders throughout North America?

MC: Yes. We all must never forget that our greatest responsibility is to help our team members and staff to develop, grow, and have better lives. We also need to have them focus on themselves and how the group needs to improve, and not get caught up in comparing ourselves to competitors. All we can control is to become the best that we can be in serving others.

DD: Just like in the restaurant business?

MC: Just like every business.

Making Michigan and Michigan State into One Team

An interview with Michele Safford

Allan Dalton: Michele, how long have you been in the real estate business?

Michele Safford: 23 years.

AD: What did you do before real estate?

MS: I was a teacher for special education.

AD: That is a blessed background, what precipitated your decision to go from being an educator to entering the real estate industry?

MS: Well, I was an educator for two years and then I was pink slipped. I then became a stay at home mom to my four children. I gradually entered real estate by first doing appraisal work in the form of secretarial type work in an office. This was beyond boring to me. Later, when we hired a gentleman named Tim to sell our home, I asked Tim if I could work for his team if I got my license. I stayed with Tim for one year.

AD: Tim must have had one of the first real estate teams in Michigan.

MS: Allan, you are exactly right, Tim was with a company named Reamerica, a Michigan brand.

AD: When you first joined Tim's team was it a conscious decision to join a team versus just joining an office and being part of that general population?

MS: Yes. I saw how an appraiser's office worked as a team, plus I figured that I would take one year to absorb everything Tim was doing, and then if I concluded that I could do these combined tasks on my own, and with my own team, then this would be best for me and my family.

AD: What did you do for Tim's team?

MS: Since my background was more clinical, I essentially provided just administrative assistance, except Tim also had me go out and do cold calling for him.

AD: The fact that you were cold calling on behalf of Tim, did this make the issue of personal rejection less personal?

MS: That is a logical question Allan, but truthfully no, rejection is still rejection.

AD: Do you still engage in so called cold calling?

MS: Not as much as I should, but I certainly do. Every good agent in my opinion should be doing cold calling and prospecting.

AD: I think it was great that you started right off doing cold calling, as many agents delay this activity for decades.

MS: I am pleased that they don't, all the more for me.

AD: Debbie De Grote tells me that you have a Master's Degree, so here you are as a very educated professional engaged in professional behavior, cold calling, which requires more courage than sophistication. How do you explain this?

MS: I recognized from my time with Tim that you have to see the people. Handing out my small business cards was clearly much more important than the size of my diplomas.

AD: When you left Tim where did you go?

MS: I actually went for 30 days to Century 21, but soon left to go to work for Paul Schweitzer, whose company was Coldwell Banker. I stayed there for 18 years and have since been with RE/MAX.

AD: At which company did you first start your team? And how many years were you in the business before you started building your team?

MS: I started while with Coldwell Banker after five years in the business.

AD: Can you walk me through the early years of your development?

MS: My first person held a clerical position. This person had worked at Ford Motor Company. She wanted to be home with her children in the summer, so I hired her for all of the other months. I witnessed firsthand how desperately I needed her when all my paperwork piled up on the floor in her absence.

AD: How soon did you brand your practice as a defined team?

MS: From when I hired that first assistant.

AD: Where and how did you start promoting your team brand name?

MS: On postcards, which I began doing massive amounts of.

AD: What was the next step in your team's organization?

MS: Buyer agents, of which I ended up hiring three since I did not enjoy working with buyers as much as sellers.

AD: So did you remain the team member handing all listing and marketing presentations?

MS: Absolutely.

AD: And this was when you were with our good mutual friend Paul Schweitzer?

MS: Yes. I would have probably stayed with Paul and Coldwell Banker forever, but Paul sold his company, so a year after he sold I moved to RE/MAX.

AD: Why did you move to RE/MAX?

MS: They had many of the better agents and were completely team supportive.

AD: Were you able to persuade your entire team to leave with you?

MS: Yes, 100%. We have always been a close knit team where everyone is respected. The one time a team member left, they decided to come back after a year, which thrilled me.

AD: Now, let's discuss how you grew your team while with the venerated RE/MAX organization.

MS: Well, I actually downsized my team a bit when I moved to RE/MAX. I ended up with just two buyer agents, one administrative person, and one additional clerical person. My administrative people share in all administrative and marketing functions from photographs, to brochures, to CMAs, to transaction management, to personal assistance.

AD: So at this time, you have two buyer agents, and all the while remaining yourself as a listing rainmaker.

MS: Correct, but now I began to encourage my buyer assistants to also list.

AD: So you now essentially have a three salesperson team all able to list, but two focused more with buyers, and you on listings.

MS: That is correct.

AD: And what would your volume be?

MS: Around $18 million.

AD: So then all of your time is exclusively with home sellers.

MS: Yes 100%. I will not even work with family buyers.

AD: What percentage of your buyer agent sales are a direct result of your listing side efforts?

MS: Approximately 90%.

AD: What percentage of your listings do they do open houses for?

MS: None. We don't do any open houses.

AD: Why not?

MS: Simply put, it is not the best use of our time.

AD: What is the name of the RE/MAX company you are with?

MS: RE/MAX Home Services.

AD: How many agents are in the firm?

MS: Allan, we are a relatively speaking small market so we only have 23 agents.

AD: How many of those 23 agents belong to teams?

MS: My best guess is all but three.

AD: And what is the name of your team?

MS: The Michele Safford Group.

AD: Why Group and not Team or Associates?

MS: Just my marketing intuition as I want to promote that our organization reflects independent professionals who work as group members as opposed to suggesting it requires a team to help someone buy a home. Plus, it sounds more like lawyers or doctors.

AD: How important do you think it is for agents to be on either a team or a group?

MS: It's vitally important. In fact, I have had homeowners tell me they eliminated certain agents as a potential listing agent because they did not belong to or have a team.

AD: Does this mean that a significant percentage of your listing presentation value proposition is about the many virtues of teams?

MS: No, my whole focus essentially still remains on me.

AD: Would you say that it is 90% you and 10% the team?

MS: No Allan, it is 98% me and 2% the team.

AD: So if you don't leverage your team, other than the 2%, and you already have a mega brand with RE/MAX, what is the major benefit of your creating your five-person team?

MS: It's all about time management and delegation. Specifically, I cannot work with buyers because they would destroy my being in control of my time. I do not want to devote time doing all of the administrative work. So creating a team has revolutionized the quality of life for me and my family. I am also proud that due to my prospecting and marketing rituals that I can generate leads for my two selling team members.

AD: It sounds as though you have a small business that requires team assistance to run properly versus you wanted to have a team that you can convert into a business.

MS: Now this one I completely agree with.

AD: How vigilant are you in following your business principles?

MS: Completely. For example, I know of some team leaders who destroy the faith of their team by telling them that they will not take any buyer leads, but then cherry pick. They will change their rules if there is a million dollar corporate transferee. I never will. I keep my word to my team, my family, and my principles.

AD: What percentage of your listings do your buyer agents sell?

MS: Only about 10%.

AD: What has been your relationship with Debbie?

MS: I met Debbie when she was a national leader in Mike Ferry's coaching operation. Debbie was actually my coach. When she left, I had several other coaches. When Debbie went out on her own I got her to promise to take me on, and she has.

AD: Does Debbie coach your team as well, or mostly you?

MS: I ask Debbie to coach me both on what I should do as a personal producer and as a team leader. I, in turn, seek to coach my agents in the same professional manner that Debbie coaches me.

AD: What else about you and your team might you share to give our readers a greater sense as to what makes you the real estate team leader you are?

MS: Thank you for that question Allan. First of all, my life does not revolve around my business, my business revolves around my life. And I want the same thing for my team members. I would like to tell you about my family. In Michigan there is an ongoing rivalry between the University of Michigan and Michigan State. Two of my four children went to The University of Michigan, which is also from where my husband graduated. Yet he and his two brothers, who all attended University of Michigan, married woman, like me, who attended Michigan State. Families, athletics, and the great outdoors represent our Michigan values. Since my clients and I share these same virtues, this sustains both my professional and personal relationships. I do not rely upon these relationships, however I constantly invest time, effort, and money into direct mail, civic events, personal promotion, and prospecting. What I am working on now is doing more business in the upscale markets. This will be the fastest way to double my business, and I am grateful that Debbie is coaching me on this process.

AD: Thank you Michele.

Radio and REO Helped This Team Get to the Top

An interview with Karey Brown

Debbie De Grote: When and why did you enter the real estate business?

Karey Brown: 2002. I wanted a career, and one that would give me the flexibility to stay with my kids. I had a seven and two year old and a newborn. An investor friend told me that I should get into real estate. I thought, how hard can it be? I laugh about that now.

DD: What did you do before real estate?

KB: I was an accountant.

DD: How did your experience in accounting influence what you have done in real estate?

KB: I got into accounting because my parents told me that I should. I'm not bad at it, I just don't enjoy it at all. It did teach me attention to detail and that is huge in real estate, especially if the other agent isn't one to pay attention to the details in the contract.

DD: Talk about your early years, which company you began with and what you did originally to set your path towards success.

KB: I started with a small local company (Kirk & Cobb) because our realtor was from that office. I was there for about six months. My father was diagnosed with cancer and real estate took a back seat to life. I had a little bit of business and had a friend cover that for me. I moved to RE/MAX because I found that I really enjoyed the broker and staff. Overall, the company was a better fit.

DD: What geographical market did you serve then and now?

KB: Starting out I was getting leads from open houses. A friend, who was also a RE/MAX agent in another city, talked me into trying REO (bank owned properties). I did, and before I knew it I had more business than I could handle. That is what got me on the "team path."

DD: Did you segment any particular market?

KB: I was told by an REO manager that I was "tech savvy, had a great sense of humor, and was a quick learner." She spread the word with other asset managers and before I knew what hit me, I was drowning in the world of REO. I learned hiring and building a team can be very difficult, especially when you have no idea how to do it. REO had provided a nice income for more than ten years of my real estate career, but when I met you, Debbie, I knew I wanted out. I just didn't know how to stop the business I had worked so hard for. You really helped me to focus on moving toward the part of the career I had originally set out to create.

DD: What percentage of your business in the early years was from listings versus sales?

KB: 70% was listings. 30% sales. I had one to two part time buyer agents at any point in time. Not really an effective way to handle what I had generated but you don't know what you don't know.

DD: When did you begin to add service staff to your personal operation?

KB: I added two part time staff right away. One to market and one to handle the REO billing.

Hindsight, I had them in the wrong roles and it cost me BIG TIME. Looking back, my marketing lady should have been the billing lady and the billing lady should have been doing the marketing. One of the most expensive lessons I learned in this business. That, and people will continue to take your money knowing they aren't doing the job. That one still baffles me.

DD: When did you officially become a team and what name did you select for it and why?

KB: I've had a team since my second year in the business. The Karey Brown Team.

DD: When you started your team, what company were you with?

KB: RE/MAX, in 2004.

DD: How many other teams were there in the company and was there any resistance to your becoming a team?

KB: There were husband and wife teams or family teams. I think maybe three.

DD: When there is resistance from brokers and company owners, what do you believe causes it?

KB: That's what I enjoyed about the broker. He was always encouraging. He knew I caught resistance from others and he tried to offset it. I hated to see him retire.

DD: Getting back to the development of your team, take me through its growth in terms of personnel, including what each function team members serve.

KB: Started with myself, two part time admin people, and a buyer agent. Graduated to the marketing and REO billing hires I mentioned before, plus a second buyer agent. Then moved to three buyer agents. I stayed at this level for several years.

Fast forward to now. I have two transaction coordinators, one listing assistant (customer service), a full time marketing assistant, one ISA, three listing agents, and four buyer agents. We are currently hiring two more ISA's and recently hired a broker to replace me [as a traditional broker]. I still run and own the company and generate business. I'm constantly trying to model after the large teams and take every opportunity to learn from them. I don't think twice about calling a large producer and asking tons of questions. The best way to learn is from those that DO!

DD: Do you consider yourself more of a team leader, team manager, or both?

KB: A little of both. I hired a broker to handle compliance and education in that aspect of the business. The rest is generated by me.

DD: Is the function of your team that team members are hired and compensated to support your efforts, or does the team exist to equally support the efforts of all team members or both?

KB: Both. My name generates a lot but our team is a tight group that supports each other. Such as buyer agents work with buyers and listing agents work with sellers. We do our best to never take away from the other side. We generate for each other.

DD: How do you differentiate your team value from the greater brokerage value of the host company?

KB: Well, we are one and the same. I own the brokerage and my team is the company.

DD: How much of your time is devoted to personally working with sellers versus buyers?

KB: By design, very little. I host a radio show, do public speaking, create our marketing plans and generate plans to move the company forward.

DD: Do you have team members who both list and sell?

KB: Four that work with buyers, three that work with sellers. None that do both. They can, but we make a point of sticking with what we enjoy so, by design, we stay on the side we are strongest in and work together as a team.

DD: Do you assign your team members geographical farms?

KB: Each buyer agent handles our local area and each works another demographic area. Listing does the same.

DD: How often does your team meet? And can you describe a typical team meeting?

KB: Once a week on Thursday's. We go through closed sales each week and each closing represents a stone that they add to their "jars." We discuss volume, where we rank in the city, marketing efforts, who is looking for what client, and what listings we have and are getting. We help each other by looking for one another's clients so we can help them find a home faster. Once a month we bring in a speaker that can help us learn in some capacity.

DD: What do you do to generate leads and which contact management system do you use?

KB: We use the typical Zillow, Realtor.com, Trulia. We get a fair amount from sphere, open houses, Facebook, referrals, and past clients. Also, our Barbara Corcoran Commercial. The local DJ endorses us, and my radio show. We are also Dave Ramsey ELP's. I've also started doing a quarterly magazine. Most recently, "Empowering Women." We also list a fair amount of business from expired listings.

Contact Management we were using Follow Up Boss and Prime Agent (Realty Executives). We are transitioning to Firepoint. It combines the three systems we were using and ties to our website.

DD: What do you think makes your team so successful?

KB: We are like a family. Everyone is of high quality character. We work hard and do our very best to make every transaction smooth for our client and other agents involved.

DD: What are some of the distinctive marketing or advertising programs you use?

KB: Zillow (as much as we love to hate them) is a great source because that is where people who don't know an agent look. We have a lot of closed sales and client referrals on the site. I love the radio show and the Barbara Corcoran commercial generates a fair amount of business also.
DD: In a sentence or two, could you describe your team's culture?

KB: We are all a very witty crew. We have a lot of fun but are all very competitive. We have a huge race track that is a visual as to where we are with our own goals. We are all very supportive of one another. If someone is running short on business (generally because they just closed a bunch) we all load them up with more.

DD: How much importance do you place on training and coaching for your team members?

KB: I'm constantly learning and sharing what I've learned with the team. I spend an hour every morning studying the teams that I'm modeling my team after. I'm constantly trying to learn something new whether it is from a book or online forums.

DD: What do you think is the biggest reason agents want to join your team?

KB: We are unique in our market. We have the highest per agent transaction count in the market and others around us. Other than that we have fun doing what we do.

DD: When and if you lose a team member, is it more likely they leave, and if so why? Or that they are let go, and if so why?

KB: We, as a team, let them go. We've only had one recently and it was a situation of the staff member not being a good fit for where we were heading.

DD: Do you allow or encourage teams within your overall team?

KB: We aren't there yet. When we get there, I'm sure we will.

DD: How important is it to your team which brokerage or brand you belong to?

KB: We are with Realty Executives. My hope is to build a coaching network with the company and teach others how to do what we do.

DD: How much volume does your team produce?

KB: Last year, just under $20 million with all brand new agents. We should double this year. That's with absolutely no REO business at all. We had cancelled all relationships in January of this year and last year we only had one REO client so we had very little in the way of REO in 2015.

DD: How do you see real estate teams evolving in the future?

KB: I think the industry is headed towards teams overall. Life is too short to take this industry on as an independent for any length of time and not have help. Someone just "covering for you" doesn't have the same desire to serve your client like your team would generally. There's still a lot to learn from some new team concepts. At least from what I see. They want to build their brand but not truly work as a team. There's a lot to learn about building a good, solid team.

DD: How has the evolution of real estate teams changed our industry?

KB: In my market we are the first that supports a team name and not just my name. I changed from The Karey Brown Team to Preferred Advisors Team. I wanted to build something that could function without me someday and pass down to my children should they decide this business is for them. I also don't do all of this on my own so I wanted my team to get the same recognition I do.

DD: Do real estate teams increase consumer service? And if so how?

KB: Absolutely! We work together on our listings and buyer clients. They don't just get one of us. They get a whole team. We are completely inter-changeable. I can be out of the country and my clients are still taken care of. Same goes for everyone on the team. We share commission with whoever covers us.

DD: Is there any question that I have not asked you that I should have to help our readers better understand what makes your team what it is?

KB: I would say in this industry a lot of agents treat their real estate career like a pass-time business. Ours is truly run like a business. We have a set amount of bills, marketing, payroll, etc. We are run like any other business and not just a "hit and miss" gig.

DD: Do you have plans on selling your team someday, and if so how will you go about that, and also what do you believe teams in general need to do to increase their value?

KB: Maybe someday if my children don't step in where I left off. I would let my team have first opportunity. As far as increasing value, the important aspects are systems, database, name recognition, and team values and reputation.

DD: How big can you see your team growing?

KB: I think I would like to get somewhere in the 25-30 people range. We do team interviews and don't just add to have head count. We have to have a need and they have to fit.

DD: How do you think the internet might change teams in the future regarding physical office space and growth?

KB: There are several teams branching out into other markets. I see this happening with our team In the future.

Working the Luxury Beach Community

An interview with Lee Ann Wilkinson

Debbie De Grote: Lee Ann, tell me what the catalyst was that caused you to make the shift from an individual producer to building and leading a team.

Lee Ann Wilkinson: In 1999, I attended a Prudential convention in Orlando, Florida where I saw Gladys Blum speaking about her production and the team she had built. At that moment it just hit me and I thought, "I need a team, this is exactly what I need to do!" At the time I was just so insanely busy that if I wanted a day off or to be able to leave at a reasonable time in order to have dinner with my kids, I had to go to work at 4:00 in the morning to get everything done. Especially during the busy season.

DD: Yes, because you are in a beach community, a resort market.

LW: Right, however our area now is so popular that we are quite busy year round.

DD: Was your first hire a strong administrative person?

LW: Yes, it actually was a lady that I knew. She was my husband's friend's wife. She had two kids that were my kids' ages, and she was a ball of fire. She had a ton of great ideas and I thought, "Yes, this is just what I need and it's going to be good!"

DD: Did she stay with you for very long?

LW: She did, she stayed with me for quite a long time and, in fact, she still works for the company.

DD: After visiting you and your market recently, I know how busy you and your teammates are. How many transactions will your team close in 2016?

LW: Over 375 units and with an average price being around $500,000.

DD: Wow! That's a lot even for a team to manage. Back in 1999 when you hired your first assistant, do you remember how many units you were doing?
LW: Probably around 50.

DD: That makes sense, as I notice that very few agents can make it past 40 or so closed units without help. Often earlier if they don't want to work around the clock as you were doing. As you were talking about the crazy early years it made me think about what a busy, single mom, top producer recently shared with me. She told me that she said to the kids often, "Which one of the 3 D's do you want for dinner tonight: delivery, drive through or just don't do it?"

LW: Yes, and as a small family business, which we were at that time, we didn't have the corporate tools and support of a large franchise, so it was all on me.

DD: Speaking of a family business, I had the pleasure of getting to know your mom and dad, Sal and Bette. They are delightful, and that's not really a word I use often. You have a wonderful and extremely productive family. What I heard from more than one family member was, "We put family first." Not always easy to do in this business, is it?

LW: No, it's not, but I try hard to make it all work.

DD: Can you tell us a little bit about how you ended up in this area and this market, maybe a bit about the history of how your family built their business?

LW: Originally we were from Pennsylvania, outside of Philly, and my grandfather had a tiny beach cottage here at Rehoboth where I spent every summer. From the time I was a little girl, my entire family would come down on the weekends. We went out on the boat, did all the fun summer activities that you would expect a family do, and just loved it. When I was about 12, my dad decided he wanted to live in the area year round, so we left our row house in Philly and moved to the beach. Except we didn't end up on the beach, instead my dad bought a 100-acre farm. We lived in the farmhouse and rented out the farmland to a local farmer and his kids.

DD: How did they move into real estate?

LW: They didn't have jobs and they needed an income. My mother had had a real estate license in Pennsylvania, although she really had only dabbled in it part time. They both got their Delaware license and went to work for Anderson Stokes, which is now Long and Foster.

DD: Ultimately though, your family decided to build their own company. What sparked that?

LW: When Mr. Stoke of Anderson Stokes passed away, things changed and weren't going so great. Most of the agents left and many, like my family, started their own companies. If you look around at most of the major brokers/companies in our market, most of them were started by agents who left when my family did. This was probably in 1980 or so.

DD: Were you in the business already?

LW: No, I was in college, and when I graduated with an art degree, I discovered I couldn't find a job that paid much. In fact, it was hard to find a job, period. So my dad said, "You can't be a waitress, you have a college degree!" I already had my license because my dad made me take the real estate class my senior year of high school. However, I had no interest in the business, absolutely none.

DD: What I heard about you though, is that once you stepped foot in the office it was game over, you were hooked. Is that true?

LW: Yes. I thought, wow this is easy, I can do this. Of course, I had grown up around salespeople, and I was selling bathing suits before I sold real estate, so I guess I had sales in the blood.

DD: We often say in the business there are hunters and skinners, you clearly are a hunter! I know your parents specialized in commercial, and I heard from a staff member that you started with rentals. Working with seasonal renters is incredibly demanding.

LW: Yes it is, but it allowed me to hone my market knowledge, allowed me to get my foot in the door and make some money without much competition. No one else wanted them so I did them. After a while though, I realized it was time to let someone else take over so that I could just focus on sales.

DD: When I drove around your area, I saw your name on signs on literally almost every street. What is your market share?

LW: At least 65% of the listings in Lewes are mine or my team's.

DD: No wonder your entire team is racing!

LW: Yes, and they are also extra busy because I demand perfection in service to our clients. I want everything to go smoothly and every client to be astounded with our excellent service. That is why we have so much repeat and referral business.

DD: How many of the 375 units are yours?

LW: A lot more than should be, but I am a control freak and Debbie, I need help to start to back off of that a little.

DD: Are you a good boss?

LW: I try to be. Everyone on my team is someone that I knew well. We are all close, and that's what makes it so tough to make a decision to bring someone else into our group. I feel we need the help at times, and then on the other hand I don't want to drain leads away from the core group I have. It's a balancing act.

DD: Yes, I know what you are saying, because you don't want to turn a positive, powerful culture into a wolf pack. It does sound though like we need to talk about some solutions for when you are overwhelmed.

LW: Yes, that's why I wanted to talk to you Debbie, I need some help with this. Plus, I should admit I am not all that anxious to have more people to manage.

DD: How many people do you have on your team?

LW: I have 15, one of them being my team manager Chris, who you met, he is terrific.

DD: He is a terrific manager, and he and his husband Emery throw a fantastic dinner party. Thank him again for me for the wonderful dinner!

LW: Yes, we treasure an invite to their house. At our own home we have Sunday night dinners. It's our thing, we make sure to make time for it!

DD: When it comes to quality time, do you take much time off?

LW: More lately, and we actually went on vacation this June, our busy season. There were a few bumps, but for the most part the team did great and all went well. I have to do it more.

DD: Okay, let's dig into a challenge I know you have, even with a great team. When you are such a dominant figure in the market you must struggle with clients insisting they only want you. Is that an issue?

LW: Yes, it's a huge issue for me, because I know if I could take every call that comes into the office I could convert them. Of course, it's not possible, but remember I told you I am a control freak. Sometimes I wonder, do I really want to jump to 475 units and beyond? Because to do that I will have to give up control. There will be a few more issues and some clients will be disappointed they don't get me.

DD: Well, that's a decision only you can make, and yet if you want to have some balance and time off, it's most likely a shift you will need to make, isn't it?

LW: Yes, I know I have to figure out how to be involved without being the point person, especially when it comes to past clients. Part of my need to perfect everything is that I am obsessed with making sure I have market knowledge, stats, everything just right before I list a property. So when I am listing in markets outside our main market, it takes more time to prepare.

DD: Many people reading this book will be deciding if they should hire a team manager. Tell them, if you will, a little about your manager Chris.

LW: I didn't really make a decision to hire a manager, Chris found me. He said, "I just retired from my business and I want to sell real estate." I didn't think he would like it, being a hunter, but he insisted on trying it. He decided after a month or two that I was right, so he wrote up his own job description and said, "This is what you need me to do for you." I said okay!

DD: If there are any newer or aspiring agents reading this book, what advice would you give them?

LW: Go to work for a team for a few years. This business is so much more aggressive and challenging than it was when I got into it and I honestly don't know how a new agent can make it. Think about it, they would be new and competing against someone like me. They should join a team, give it their all, do a good job, and learn. Then later if they choose to, they can go out on their own.

DD: You are part of a real estate family; do you hire family to work on your team?

LW: I do. In fact, I am thinking of hiring my goddaughter, and I'm nervous. I always worry that something might go wrong.

DD: Yes, and yet you have built such a wonderful business it would be a shame not to share it with those you love, right?

LW: Yes, you're right.

DD: Is there a special profile you look for when you hire team members? For example, one of the teams showcased in this book, Stanfield Real Estate, likes to hire young, aggressive, and well-connected people in the area. Anything you look for in particular?

LW: No, I wish I could say that I do, but I am not that good at picking people. I often pick the wrong people, and then I have to fire them. I think I need some help from you with this too Debbie.

DD: Again, this is very common, which is why I wrote the book *The Real Estate Agent's Complete Guide to Hiring, Training, and Retaining Top Talent*. Because most of our clients need help with this.

DD: Question for you if you are comfortable answering, is there anything you would share about the splits you pay your team?

LW: I want to get my team on a unified plan, but right now I have most of them on different splits and plans, which gets kind of messy. I find myself in a pinch cutting deals here and there randomly, deal to deal.

DD: As a coach this is something I work to stop clients from doing because it almost always leads to hard feelings and extra work and stress to negotiate it. Best not to do this.

LW: Yes, I need to stop doing that, I just get caught up in the moment.

DD: You know at Excelleum we coach some of the best teams in the nation, and everyone who comes to us would say they have gaps they need help with, so you're not alone. Switching gears for a minute, where does most of your business come from?

LW: 65% of it is repeat and referral, and the rest just from people who know or see my name and call in.

DD: I guess that is the side benefit of having signs all over town. I know a big portion of your property owners are second home owners, or absentees. Do you market to them?

LW: Yes, we have for years and years by mail, very faithfully.

DD: Is open house popular in your market?

LW: No they don't work for us at all. Nobody comes, they go to the beach.

DD: You have shared some great points with our readers, just one or two last questions. Do you have any big goals for the year ahead?

LW: To have a bit more time off, to do 475 deals in 2017, and to maybe do a few more higher-end properties.

DD: You are a woman of action, I know you can make it happen. I look forward to talking to Chris soon about how we can help you get there. You are such a pleasure and an inspiration! Thank you for taking time to talk to me today.

LW: You are welcome, it was fun!

Building a Bigger and More Profitable Team That You Can Sell!

By Debbie De Grote

Why is it that medical and legal teams and partnerships seem to have far greater success in selling their businesses than real estate teams and groups?

One reason is that they live in the world of their clients being lifetime clients, not just during a transaction, as is often the case with real estate professionals. Another reason is that they develop strategies much earlier on for the cessation of their businesses. Following are some of my recommendations for building a saleable business.

"The only reason to build a business is to sell it." – Michael Gerber

1. In order to build a saleable business you must have well defined systems and processes that the average staff member/agent can follow. You cannot build your business depending on rock star talent.
2. You need to define the roles of the team clearly – including job descriptions and schedules.
3. You need to have one on one meetings and systems to keep them in check and accountable and monitor the progress.
4. Everyone needs to own their role and they need to also be cross trained to cover for each other.
5. You must identify and develop your culture.
6. Hire slowly and fire quickly.
7. Any changes you make to the system must be immediately documented and updated in your systems manual. Do a thorough clean up each December to start the year fresh.
8. Have expectations and standards and make them clear.
9. Follow carefully the guidelines for independent contractors vs. employees.
10. Track the money! Monitor expenses and profit – review P and L monthly.
11. Define what you do and who you need to replace you.
12. You must have strong methods for attracting, converting, and closing leads.
13. Building and managing the database is the life blood of the business.

14. Identify your weaknesses and get help to correct them or hire coverage to do them for you.
15. Track billable time of salespeople – 50% of their day should be income producing with a goal to reach 80%.
16. Pay close attention to customer complaints – where there is smoke there may be fire. Strive to exceed expectations and wow with service.
17. Have a system to win referrals and everyone on the team should participate.
18. Have scripts, checklists, and trackable processes for all you do.
19. Have and use efficiently a decent CRM.
20. Extend your team by developing a group of quality affiliates to work closely with and be loyal.
21. Work yourself out of a job, if the business depends on you then you don't truly have a business, you have a job. (from *The E-Myth*, by Michael Gerber)
22. Establish the vision up front: Where do you want to end up? What do you want from the sale?
    a. Complete and full transfer – up front cash and gradual pay out.
    b. Partial transfer – you act as CEO and guide the ship in a limited fashion.
    c. What are the financial rewards you can expect?
23. Develop your timeline and action steps to get there – a gradual transition plan.
24. Determine when and how to bring in your replacement.
25. Establish and document strong hiring practices (see my book *The Real Estate Agent's Complete Guide to Hiring, Training, and Retaining Top Talent*).
26. The contract you will need to pass the baton.
27. How you will audit the profits post sale to insure you receive adequate compensation.
28. You must be profitable!

This is the brass ring, to first build a business that allows the team leader to leverage their time and talent, then to allow them to focus on the aspects of the business they most enjoy while delegating the rest, and then, ultimately, having a business that is a true asset that will fund their retirement and leave a legacy behind for their team to continue to grow and prosper.

It's certainly a worthwhile vision, and yet it's a hard road to get there and often requires a host of mentors and consultant to help aggressive entrepreneurs like you to avoid costly mistakes, perfect the systems, and fast track success.

Please know that the Excelleum team has many years of experience in the buying, selling and merging of real estate franchises and companies, and are here to help you strategize on how to build a more saleable business.

I would welcome your comments and stories and if you have an interest in finding out more about how the faculty at Excelleum can support you in your growth reach out to us and we will schedule a complimentary conversation to begin the steps to your real estate future.

If you would like to learn more about how to recruit, hire, train and retain your team members look for my book *The Real Estate Agent's Complete Guide to Hiring, Training, and Retaining Top Talent.* It's a complete reference and resource guide, a must have, and a priceless resource!

If you would like to speak to me or one of my wonderful coaches from my experienced faculty of coaches simply reach out to us.

Message to Brokers:

Questions you may want our help answering…

> Q: What are other brokers doing to stop real estate teams from consolidating commission splits of team members by rolling everyone into the team leaders splits?
> Q: What are the resources I can and should provide to retain the teams I have and to encourage even more teams to join me?
> Q: How can I stop teams from diluting our culture?
> Q: How can I stop teams from using and abusing my corporate staff?
> Q: How do I manage their desire to brand the team vs. the company?
> Q: How can I help them take their team to the next level, especially when they don't seem willing to change?

These are just a few of the questions that brokers bring to us on a regular basis.

If, as a broker, you need some help we would be happy to schedule a complimentary strategy call for you with one of our leadership coaches.

A Team Reaching for the Sky

An interview with Marny Schlopy

Debbie De Grote: Marny, as the founder and absolute leader of Team Schlopy, when did you first come into the real estate business?

Marny Schlopy: 1992.

DD: And when did you start your team?

MS: 1995. I hired my first assistant and shared her with another agent. I did this because I was doing enough transactions that I could now afford this, and I recognized that for me to grow and do much more business that this would be necessary.

DD: And what does your team look like today in terms of members and staff?

MS: Well, after being in business for ten years myself, my husband Kent joined me in 2002. This was right after the Salt Lake City Winter Olympics. Then right after this our son-in-law Kevin Crockett, who moved from Los Angeles with my daughter and our grandchild, also joined my real estate operation. Also of great significance is that my son Erik joined the Schlopy Real Estate Team in July of 2014.

DD: Please trace this team evolution from the beginning to now once more.

MS: Well, I went from being a single agent in 1992 to hiring a part time assistant in 1995, to then having two assistants when my husband joined me in 2002, to then hiring my son-in-law later in 2002, to where now with the addition of both my son and son-in-law. I have four full service realtors, one buyer agent named Lana, and three support people.

DD: What do your three support people do?

MS: Linda Howard is my office manager. She answers the phones, processes my listings, and handles the Docusigns. She is the person who crosses the t's and dots the i's, as they say.

DD: Would you describe her as your right hand person?

MS: Yes. Then there is Wendy Martin. Wendy does a tremendous job for our team as the Director of Client Relations and she assists us with all of our under contracts to closing. She is the person who excels at client care. She also calls our database and works with anyone who needs a little hand holding.

DD: In writing this book, I do so with the intent of providing growing teams of all sizes with hundreds of ideas and thoughts from the teams we interview and the perspective of myself and Allan Dalton. An example of this is how you just mentioned that Wendy is your Director of Client Relations. I am convinced that after reading our book that next year more teams will change the title of someone on their staff to Director of Client Relations. It is so much more sophisticated and leverage-able than many of the titles we see within teams. I love how it signals how you honor and serve your clients. It almost makes a person want to be a client, just because it sounds as though your team has set up a division just for them, I love it.

MS: That's exactly the idea, and that's exactly how Wendy makes everyone else feel.

DD: Without naming names, because we really try to keep the names of staff out of our interviews, given how this can change, what do your other staff people do?

MS: One works on buyer lead generation and the other on social media management.

DD: What does the social media staff person do for the team?

MS: 24 hours a day she has set up systems to capture leads that come in from our website and social media platforms.   And then the last person we hired is our Director of Marketing. He handles all of our marketing, and what's great is how Tyler is also proficient in handling our drone technology.

DD: What is Tyler's background?

MS: He comes to our team from a marketing background.

DD: Well, that leaves Marny, Kent, Erik, and Kevin. What do you and your other three family team members do?

MS: We are a well-coordinated sales team. We do the selling.

DD: How do you position your team's resources and structure as a benefit to prospective home sellers?

MS: That we provide home sellers with immediate care and constant communication. That the home sellers do not have to fear that their listing agent will be off working as a buyer agent for three days, and that we are constantly looking to get their property sold and are always immediately available to them.

DD: How do the four selling team members pay for the administrative staff?

MS: Well, let me do the overall picture. The four partners are equal partners. Our son-in-law, for example, had to generate $150,000 of commissions before becoming a partner. Once someone becomes a partner, we are all completely equal partners so we get a salary. My husband, who has a fantastic business and administrative background, handles the finances. We also all get a car allowance and equally share all expenses. Then at the beginning of July and January we split all profits equally.

DD: You mention that your husband handles the finances - who is the strategic leader of the business if you had to say one being more so than any other?

MS: That would be me I guess, as the founder. But we all contribute to the strategy and execution. We have two-day off site retreats, for example, where we completely reexamine everything we are doing, where we constantly make adjustments and improvements of our team plan. There is no one dominant leader as we all have our own areas of expertise and we function well.

DD: It seems like you have structured your team more along the lines of a law firm with general partners, than a conventional top down real estate team or group. Is that an accurate assessment on my part?

MS: Yes, that is an excellent analogy, but I should say that although we are four equal partners, when there is any impasses between the four of us the other partners expect me, as the founding partner, to assume the role of the ultimate managing partner and make decisions in order to prevent inaction or deadlock. However, we all collaborate and none of us, including me, dictates.

DD: Do you think it is easier to arrive at this four equal-partner arrangement because you are essentially a family team?

MS: Not because we are a family, but rather because we are a family that not only loves each other but loves to work and play together. In many cases this type of arrangement would be more difficult within a family. It still requires that all partners be able to put egos aside, work collaboratively, and not be greedy. And to above all put the value to our clients first.

DD: Plus, isn't Utah legendary for strong families?

MS: Yes, but we are not from Utah. My husband and I are from the East Coast, and our son-in-law, as I mentioned, is from California.

DD: Getting back to Utah, how big is your local market, and what is your average sales price?

MS: About 50,000 residents and average sales price of about $600,000.

DD: How much does your being a Sotheby's affiliate help you with that average sales price?

MS: Where Sotheby's helps us most is with the multimillion dollar sales. However, 70% of our business is from our personal referrals and existing relationships.

DD: Sotheby's is a phenomenal brand so let me ask you this... How much of your success is due to the Sotheby's brand versus you and your team brand?

MS: Almost all of our success is due to the hard work, systems, and services generated by our team over the years. Otherwise everyone with the same brand would all do the same amount of business and that is not the case. As I said, most of our success is due to what our team brand and our personal local value represent.

DD: How does the development of a real estate team benefit your personal lives?

MS: Immeasurably. It means that while my husband and I are far from retirement, having a team makes it possible to do things like travel to China, a medical mission to Haiti, our bike trip to Italy, or getting to enjoy our home in St. George more frequently.

DD: Let's be even more specific. How many weeks a year are you now able to enjoy due to being part of a trusted team with other partners and four full time support people?

MS: I would say ten weeks, which would be impossible for someone who is not part of a team, or who runs a team.

DD: You say your partners, your family, also like playing together.

MS: We are a total ski family. Our son is a three time Olympian, a seven time national champ, and a bronze medalist in the world championship. And our grand kids are great little skiers, although they are also big time into soccer and track.

DD: How does your team court out of state owners, considering you are in a resort area?

MS: Debbie, it is interesting you ask that. First of all, we did an analysis this year which I thought was quite revealing. We studied how many of our clients were local versus who still lived out of area and it was 50/50. The income we generated from each sector was also 50/50. This just reinforced why we had to be prominent through Google search and also why we had to be obsessed with getting immediately back to all buyers, thus our social media and marketing staff.

DD: How many associates are there in Park City?

MS: 90.

DD: If your broker was not wise enough to allow you to function as a team, and I think you have a world class broker and Brand there, would you have stayed?

MS: I agree with your descriptions of each, but in a word, no. We would have been forced to leave, obviously.

DD: How many teams are there within your Park City Sotheby's brokerage?

MS: About ten. Some two people, others four in total.

DD: How do you differentiate yourselves from other teams in your market?

MS: Our customer care and white glove service. Our client care systems.

DD: How do you think you benefit your Sotheby's International Realty local company?

MS: Well, beyond bringing listings, by helping them promote greater overall company results and market share. We made them $400,000 last year.

DD: What is your overall volume?

MS: We will sell about $75 million this year.

DD: That is amazing in a market of only 50,000 people. My basic market, Huntington Beach, has over 200,000 people, and right next store Long Beach has over 400,000. I am impressed.

MS: But what has always been impressive to me Debbie, is how you, my coach, were selling over 100 homes a year in that crazily competitive Orange County market when you were in your 20's, so right back at you. Plus, you are so instrumental in our success.

DD: Why do you think teams are continuing to evolve at such a rapid rate?

MS: I think more than anything it has to do with the web. Today's internet related generations want immediate responsiveness and service. And it is not only the millennials, it is becoming everyone. If the leaders of the industry and individual agents are honest with themselves, how can an individual agent, when they are spending hours with one buyer, possibly be simultaneously equally vigilant regarding responding to a seller or other buyer?

Top producing agents do not want to turn their clients over to a system within their larger company where they lose control, or where their meticulously developed systems are not completely adhered to. Therefore, who suffers? Customers and clients, and when customers and clients suffer, the realtor suffers.

This is a reality that will make the future of teams even more prominent. The future of real estate teams will be driven by the future of consumer expectations.

Editor's note:

At the time of the interview Marny and her team were with Sotheby's International Realty. Team Schlopy decided in May 2016 to move to Coldwell Banker Residential Brokerage to enhance their team brand.

From Loan Officer to Real Estate Team Leader

An interview with Rob Buffington

Debbie De Grote: Rob, thank you for participating in *Building Bigger, Busier, and More Profitable Teams*. Let me begin by asking you, when did you start your team and what is your brand name?

Rob Buffington: I started my team in 2013 and our name is the Buffington Real Estate Group.

DD: Why Group and not Team and/or Associates?

RB: I really didn't give it much thought Debbie. In fact, I have a mentor who works out of New York who has been pretty successful with what he calls a group. I liked the ring of it. That said, I have changed my corporate name to Buffington and Associates. Although I have not as of yet implemented that name as part of our marketing pieces. It is something I am working on right now. We will ultimately become the Buffington and Associates Real Estate Group, but will still function as a group.

DD: I know you are a newly formed and smaller group, which is helpful for our book. I want to capture all different sizes of groups and teams from different markets, cities, suburbs, and, in fact, two countries, America and Canada. So let me ask, how many members comprise your group?

RB: There are five professionals within our group. Four are active agents, along with a back office administrator.

DD: Rob, I know from our coaching with you that you are a former loan officer. What did you learn as a loan officer that has helped shape what you have done in real estate?

RB: The first thing it taught me that I have applied to real estate is to understand all that it takes for a buyer prospect to be able to buy a home. My background, which I explain to buyers, enables me to more rigorously qualify them as well as cause them to be more realistic. This is huge from a time management process. My background also helps me select the right loan officers for my buyers and to stay on top of everything from application to closing.

DD: Do you leverage your background as a loan officer with home sellers by pointing out how you provide an additional layer of buyer qualification?

RB: Probably not as much as I should. Instead, I essentially just try to leverage my overall success, because nothing sells like success.

DD: I know you only have two years under your belt but how much business do you expect to close in your third year?

RB: We are on pace for $25 million Debbie.

DD: Rob, what was your motivation in forming your group?

RB: I got to a point where I started to see the market shift and I had more leads than I could personally handle. I realized that I needed help in the form of administration and a buyer agent. I concluded that the three things I wanted to focus on almost exclusively every day were listing presentations, negotiating contracts, and prospecting. And I wanted to delegate everything else. I also wanted to, instead of spending 18 hours with a buyer and two hours with a seller, to spend much more time with sellers and delegate the buyers. However, I do still spend about 35% of my time with buyers. I guess that's the former loan officer in me.

DD: How does the team split regarding buyers and sellers?

RB: We did 80 transactions last year, 50 with sellers and 30 with buyers.

DD: Had your broker discouraged you from starting your group, what would you have done?

RB: Fortunately, my broker and I have worked out how we can mutually benefit one another, so I didn't have to leave the company to form a group.

DD: What is the name of the company you work for?

RB: Tomie Raines.

DD: I read about your company and it seems as though there are a lot of teams. Did this also influence your decision to go to market as a group?

RB: Great observation Debbie, indeed it did.

DD: How does your group benefit the overall company?

RB: We are the top team at Tomie Raines. This means that we not only drive listings to the company, but since a lot of company agents specialize with buyers, we drive business to them. In fact, this keeps them in the business and allows them to also get occasional listings from their spheres of influence.

DD: What other ways does your team contribute to the greater company?

RB: Tomie Raines has a mentoring program and I personally mentor some of the newer agents to the company.

DD: Was there any initial resistance from the company when you decided to form a group?

RB: Yes, but only a little, and I completely understood and respected why. A lot of it was space related issues. And, of course, the other issue had to do with how the business done by group members would be treated through my higher commission split. All of the group member transactions were credited at the board as from Rob Buffington. Therefore, the broker has to deal with the fact that all of our business would be treated at a higher commission split than it would be if it the transactions were unbundled.

DD: Well, why wouldn't the broker be upset or concerned with this result?

RB: It only works for the broker when the team does enough business. The team absorbs other costs, the team assumes the training and recruiting efforts and the costs. When the team generates greater market share and results, that in turn benefits the entire company.

DD: In your marketing material you use two expressions: specialists and uncommon service. Explain.

RB: They are specialists in that some work with buyers, others sellers. Additionally, we work hard at developing our skill level and are completely dedicated to providing uncommon service. As we know we do by the raves and reviews of our clients. While it is difficult to quantify service, we are obsessed as a group in the level of service we offer, it defines us.

DD: How much accountability do you introduce with your small group?

RB: I try to constantly encourage my teammates and not brow beat them. We go over their goals every Monday, and they know how important it is for the sake of the entire group that we hit these numbers.

DD: Although you are only a few years as a group leader, what, if anything, do you regret to date?

RB: Not hiring an administrator and buyer agent immediately. Also, hiring four administrators before realizing that I needed to follow the DISC process.

DD: Do you have the right one now?

RB: Absolutely and I must share her name as I am so proud of her professionalism. My current administrator is Hattie Cable.

DD: Rob, we have the privilege of coaching your team here at Excelleum. Who is your coach?

RB: Wally. He is absolutely the best. The guidance, ideas, and strategies we review together are instrumental in what I do and how I coach my teammates.

DD: How do you leverage your group during listing presentations?

RB: We liken our group to a medical group where the homeowner has both the equivalent of a primary doctor, as well as the team of specialists. So the person who does brochures is like our XRAY technician, etc.

DD: Is there any conflict between company and group branding?

RB: Yes, as it is inevitable, and I am sure it exists across North America with the exponential explosion of real estate teams. We work it out though, because there is an underlying mutual respect.

DD: Is coaching more important to you as an individual or as a group leader?

RB: I would say to me as a group leader. Wally helps with my profit and loss statement, holds me accountable, and breaks down with me the role of everyone on our teams. He also involves the DISC program so we all understand our strengths and weaknesses and how to grow as a group.

DD: One of my greatest focuses as a coach and as CEO of my coaching and consulting company is to help instill confidence in all with whom I work. So speaking of confidence, let me ask you this: has developing a group created more confidence in you, Rob?
RB: Debbie, confidence is a major concept in my life and career as well. So let me speak to it.

First off, by virtue of simply developing a group, it has significantly increased my confidence. It has also confirmed for me that I have the abilities, strategic mind, work ethic, and commitment to serve that has led me to growing from that of an individual agent into a true business leader.

My confidence is greater because I now know that when I meet home sellers and buyers that no service issue will fall between the cracks. This is because I have instituted, along with my group's high level servicing systems, superior marketing. Consequently, my confidence is brimming when I hand out my card that shows that we are a group, and I am the leader of the group.

I know my group members all have more confidence due to our published results and the knowledge we all gain from one another.

DD: Rob, tell me about this process of learning from one another.

RB: One of the benefits and great rewards of having a group is how it leads to the highest degrees of trust and sharing possible. Our group meetings represent our locker room, so to speak. As a result, nothing leaves the locker room, and we are all completely bonded on these assumptions. I make it a point at each meeting to have everyone openly and candidly share what is positive and negative. Everyone gets to share everything they think is appropriate.

You just cannot duplicate this in an office meeting, company meeting, or industry meeting. This team dynamic provides a true family atmosphere and it makes being in business, and real estate itself, so much more meaningful than just trying to make money.

DD: Speaking of family, do you have children?

RB: Well, now you are talking about the ultimate group or team: my family, which would be my beloved wife and four children. My family represents my why for all I do.

DD: Thank you Rob, for providing another perspective of a successful real estate team.

Mario Plus Miguel Equals More

An interview with Mario Chirino & Miguel Solis

Allan Dalton: How did you get into real estate? First you, Miguel, and then you, Mario, and what is your personal relationship with one another?

Miguel Solis: I got into the real estate profession in the early 2000s, and with my personality I thought it would be a good fit.

Mario Chirino: I worked in sales before real estate and felt like real estate would be the next step for me. It felt like it would be the right fit at the right time. We met each other working in real estate at Prudential Florida Realty and have worked together now for ten years.

AD: Which company did you start with?

MS: Coldwell Banker.

MG: Prudential Florida Realty.

AD: How long did you sell as individuals before hiring an assistant?

M/M: For the last ten years we have not had assistants because we were each other's assistants. In the last five years we have brought on another assistant that takes on more of a role in marketing.

AD: It's interesting what you say. So essentially, you functioned as a partnership where each one of you was the other individual's assistant. I don't know if I've ever heard a partnership put quite that way. But I love it, because it shows that both of you possess both leadership and the all-important quality of servitude. Now let me ask you, how did each of you do individually?

M/M: We have always been top producing agents in real estate. Thus, we got together in order to make more business happen and cover each other's bases. To us, the most solid team is a partnership where two equal individuals possessing different strengths and weaknesses both complement, as well as compliment each other.

AD: I love it. When did you start your team and what is the name?

M/M: The name of the team is Solis Chirino Group. It was started ten years ago when the real estate market turned. At that time we both felt it was needed and it took off from there.

AD: What role does each of you assume?

MS: I assume more of a role of new business ventures and bringing in new business.

MC: While I oversee the daily follow ups, deadlines, contracts, and making appointments. We both show properties and aid in the buying and selling of homes.

AD: What percentage of your time is spent on selling?

M/M: 24/7, anytime, anyplace.

AD: What percentage of your business is listings versus sales?

M/M: 50% to 50%.

AD: What geographical markets do you serve?

M/M: Dade County, Broward County, and a splash of Monroe County.

AD: What percentage of your clients speaks both Spanish and English?

M/M: 75% speak both English and Spanish, 20% only speak English, and 5% only speak Spanish.

AD: What do you see as the benefits of a team to the consumers, both buyers and sellers?

M/M: More availability in order to successfully market, show listings/properties to buyers, as well as showcase and sell and find the property that the clients are looking for. Twice the knowledge. The real estate consumers that we serve completely grasp how they benefit from having two great agents instead of just one good one representing them, and at basically the same fee.

AD: I love that. Two great agents, instead of one good one, at basically the same fee. That sounds like it would be a great ad. Although, I don't know if you could get into the subject of commissions quite that way.

M/M: The reason why we like this message is that by referring to our competition as a good agent, it is very respectful, but we must remember that there is a big difference between one good agent and two great ones.

AD: What are the benefits to you both professionally and personally by teaming up?

M/M: Overall real estate knowledge, availability, and great reputation built over time. Personally, we are both bilingual and both have great communication skills as well as being very personable. We also provide each other with personal time that would not be available to either one of us if we just operated as individual, top-producing agents.

AD: Who provides more resources to your team, yourself or your company?

M/M: Both provide resources to our team, and when you add it up it creates the perfect mix to be successful in real estate. Just as we see each other as partners to one another, we consider our team as an equal partner to our company. And our company's CEO instills a spirit of teamwork, as does our office manager, throughout our whole company and our office.

AD: Are teams in Florida becoming much more prominent, and if so why?

M/M: Yes, we are seeing more and more teams. Teams are able to be in several locations at the same time and have more versatility. We also have different people to choose for the right job.

AD: Does the fact that you serve a multi-cultural market make having a team even more beneficial?

M/M: We find that our Spanish-speaking clients value how we are also fluent in English because they want access to the entire diverse market we serve. And those that we serve who speak English indicate they feel exactly the same way. So in a sense, we are not just a real estate twosome, we are a twosome when it comes to the primary languages we speak. But this is nothing unusual, as our Hispanic clients not only are a very sizable population in America, but in many of our markets we represent the majority. We should also say that while there may be differences in various cultures, in terms of preference in food, entertainment, religion, etc., all people want the same thing. If they're selling their home they want the highest price and if they are buying a home they want to find their dream home and not overpay.

AD: I don't see how anybody could disagree with that. How much business does your team do?

M/M: Approximately $25 million annually.

AD: How often do you meet?

M/M: We meet every Wednesday and Friday for marketing meetings, also we are always in continuous contact.

AD: What distinctive services does your partnership provide consumers over and above what the company provides?

M/M: Customized marketing, graphic design, new innovative ideas, social marketing, multimedia presentations.

AD: It sounds as though you not only have the linguistics well covered, but that you are a major force when it comes to the visuals and real estate imagery.

M/M: Absolutely Allan. Florida is a very visual and an even, if you will, sensual marketplace. Our ecology is mesmerizing and we are both committed to capturing this in the way we visually portray our lifestyles.

AD: How large do you want to grow your team?

M/M: We are always open to adding support staff but we prefer, to any degree possible, that the face to face professional service provided to buyers and sellers comes from one of the two of us.

AD: Do you believe that team members receive more career development help by virtue of being on a team in general?

M/M: Yes, there are a lot of benefits attained from being on a team like accountability, responsibilities, and structure. These benefits can help in many aspects of life.

AD: Do you think having created a team will make it more likely that someday you might be able to sell your business?

M/M: Yes, by being on a team we have brought in a lot more clients than if we were not working together. Although we are a team we both are constantly prospecting for new business.

AD: What are some of the things you do to market yourself and your team locally?

M/M: Social media, agent mailing (mail out), expired listing communications, American Lifestyle Magazines to our clients, e-blasts to all of our contacts.

AD: What makes you successful as a team?

M/M: Knowledge of the market. Appeal to clientele with representation of the highest professionalism that is demanded by Berkshire Hathaway and the Chairman and CEO Warren Buffett. We at Solis Chirino Group understand that the real estate business is not only a profession, but a way of life.

AD: Thank you very much, Mario and Miguel, for really enforcing the importance and the success reflected in two-person teams/partnerships. There are thousands of such teams in the industry and as I can see in this interview, the absolute common thread is and must be mutual respect.

M/M: Allan we could not agree more and thank you and Debbie De Grote so much for including us in the book.

A Broker's Balanced Views on Teams

An interview with Rei Mesa

Allan Dalton: Rei, the reason why Debbie De Grote asked me to interview you for the book is to gain the perspective of one of America's leading brokers, leading a 40-plus office company, regarding the impact of real estate teams in your organization. So let me begin with your background.

Rei Mesa: Well, I have been in the industry for 35 years. I began as a sales professional at the age of 18, I have worked as a branch manager, broker owner, regional vice president, and for the past 12 years as President and CEO of Berkshire Hathaway HomeServices Florida Realty.

AD: What is the precise size of your organization and which markets are you in?

RM: Our Family of Services has 42 locations serving 19 Florida counties with 1,800 sales professionals and over 250 employees.

AD: Is your company owned by HomeServices or are you locally and individually owned?

RM: We are an independently owned and operated franchisee of Berkshire Hathaway HomeServices.

AD: Well, this interview will probably not be as long as most of our book interviews because you are not leading a real estate team in the contemporary and conventional sense or meaning of the term.

RM: What do you mean? I am leading a real estate team of 1,800 sales professionals and 250 employees with a sales volume of $3.1 billion in 2015. I thought that was the premise of this interview.... only kidding Allan.

AD: Trust me Rei, I have similarly joked about myself and my 20 years as President and co-owner of a 32 office firm, but we both know that is not what the industry, real estate companies, or this book represents regarding real estate teams.

RM: Yes, I am well aware of what real estate teams now represent.

AD: So let me get right to the point. What are your views, your policy, and your philosophy about real estate teams in general, and specifically within your own organization?

RM: They are complex, and I don't think I am the only broker who feels that way. In fact, I know I am not.

AD: You seem quite certain of your assertion.

RM: And for good reason. I had the privilege of being appointed by the National Association of Realtors© as the 2012 Large Firm liaison. During these meetings there was much discussion between official meetings, over dinner, etc. regarding the increasing emergence of real estate teams. Specifically, a lot of my broker colleagues and friends shared their perspective regarding the formation of teams from a cultural, financial, and general brokerage liability stand point.

AD: Then who better than you, both from the stand point of your own brokerage as well as from all of the brokers you informally discussed the subject of real estate teams with, to interview? Thus, what are you feelings and what did you learn from throughout the industry?

RM: Well, first let me be clear that my views are just that, my own. I do not speak for The National Association of Realtors©, Berkshire Hathaway HomeServices, nor any other brokerage. Let me start with my sense from the community of brokerages.

AD: Sounds good, what did you learn?

RM: Some are completely in favor and promote real estate teams, and have decided to build their brokerages or brands through this business model. It is not that they will not allow individual agents, it's just that they want it to be known that they are real estate team centric brokers.

AD: What was the attitude or stance of most of the large brokers?

RM: I would say there were three categories. One, some either emphatically discouraged teams, although this was four years ago, and I see that some have softened that position. Two, some had the following attitude: "We don't like the idea... but we have to selectively support and embrace it. The reality is that real estate teams are here to stay." And third, there were some who thought it was a good way to keep top producers by shifting some of their marketing and training costs and essentially preventing some of their better agents from joining other companies who were seen as more team friendly.

AD: Now let's get to your views Rei.

RM: The first part of my views I know I share with almost every large company broker and most small company and mid-size brokers as well. That many individuals who look to start real estate teams are completely either ignorant or insensitive to the economics of running a complete and incorporated business. They, therefore, are actually surprised to learn why many brokers are concerned over this trend.

AD: Speak to the economics Rei.

RM: There has been an established economic equilibrium that has been observed for decades, which some real estate team leaders seemed intent on ignoring.

AD: Specifically?

RM: The broker/owner or company would assume all of the financial expenses (i.e. location cost of the office, assume all the liability, pay for almost all of the overhead, and with all that just manage to make a small percentage of the gross commission income). These margins were tough even when commission splits were for many years 50/50 for everyone.

Then we experience a significant change of commission splits in order to compete with new business models and retain top producers, which I have always respected because top producers, like star athletes, deserve every penny of what they can get paid.

The challenge is that when some of these team leaders want to aggregate all of their far less producing sales professionals into their much more favorable commission splits then this is where many brokers feel they are at a financial disadvantage.

So to me real estate teams are a great movement. The good ones can provide great coordinated services, train new sales professionals, and help the company bring in a lot more listings and credibility, which helps the whole company.

Where they could be harmful and not acceptable is when they do not strive to work out a fair and balanced financial arrangement and expense sharing relationship with the brokerage.

AD: It sounds like you approve and completely respect teams when they establish a symbiotic and not a parasitic relationship with the host brokerage, if you will.

RM: Yes, and that is the view of many leading brokerages. Real estate teams should work in complete harmony with the brokerage / company, which is our complete aim as a company. But it has to be two-sided support with a win-win goal in mind. Such teams need to help the company, not divide it. And don't expect a broker to spend a fortune to create a brand respected brokerage by investing a small fortune over the years, and then come in and say you are a company within the company, but look to make more from the company than the broker through violating the basic premise behind progressive commission splits.

It would be like LeBron James saying that all the other players on the team were now part of his compensation and the team owner is going to pay LeBron the same amount of money for their baskets as the ones he scores.

AD: Other than the financial aspects when they get out of hand, are you in favor of real estate teams?

RM: Allan, it's not that simple. Here is what I am in favor of: I encourage every sales professional in our company to take every possible means to best provide for themselves and their families. I also want each and every sales professional in our company to know that we spend a great deal of time and resources so that each and every sales professional that joins our company is already on a great team, the company team. We hire highly capable branch managers, regional vice presidents, and support staff who they should also view as teammates or partners. That they do not need to join a team to receive the full developmental attention they so richly deserve.

I support how some of our sales professionals can accelerate their career developmental process by enjoying the more experienced mentoring from a specific real estate team leader. And I also support those sales professionals who do not want to be confined to the structure of a team or group and want to experience the methods and systems suggested by the larger company and brand.

Therefore, at the end of the day, as CEO of the company, my passion is that everyone in the company, from realtor associates who join teams, to those who don't, to our mangers and executive team members, to our mortgage and title partners, we are all part of one big team, Berkshire Hathaway HomeServices Florida Realty.

You see, Florida is known for its diverse people and markets, so diversity of business models are most welcome by me and our company. But it must be fair for everyone, and at our company it is.

AD: Therefore, you would be in a great position to articulate the views that many expressed about real estate teams.

RM: Yes, but my perspective was not from the meetings themselves, rather from the numerous breakfast, lunch, and dinner informal discussions. This is where the subject often comes up.

AD: Indeed, as those would be opportune times to get a true feel for views and opinions. Thank you Rei, for this thought-provoking interview and for taking the time to be a part of this book.

The Team of All Teams: The National Association of Realtors©

An interview with Charlie Oppler

Allan Dalton: Charlie, when Debbie De Grote and I reached out to you to get your perspective on real estate teams I was surprised by your reaction. Specifically because you are the broker/owner of a major real estate company within the Realogy family of brands, have served as a VP of the National Association of Realtors©, as well as a liaison for the large size brokers for the NAR, and we thought that you would have much to share regarding real estate teams and groups as commonly understood. Of significance is how you, instead, wanted to take my question of the importance of teams in another direction.

Charlie Oppler: Allan, as you know, team and teamwork is one of my great passions in life. I came close to being a major league pitcher, and played basketball on numerous teams. Therefore, the concept of teams and teamwork is in my blood. Since Debbie De Grote and yourself have decided to write about teams, I sensed that it would be about real estate teams and groups that have been formed over the past decade or so within brokerages. Now, while I have encouraged and worked with husband and wife teams, international teams, and teams comprised of top producers who have assistants, team buyers, and listing specialists within my company, I am sure your book will already have that subject well covered. I think your book would have a major void, however, if it doesn't also devote at least some attention to the most important team in the industry: The National Association of Realtors©.

AD: Why is the National Association of Realtors© the most important team?

CO: Let me count the ways. First of all, one of the reasons is that our team, the National Association of Realtors© team, if you will, enables consumers to transact billions of dollars in a state of complete trust of their real estate decision, because all REALTORS© commit to a code of ethics. Therefore, consumers trust our team.

AD: Elaborate on the importance of that please.

CO: Well, imagine what it would be like if we needed to have a million real estate licensees all having to individually, independently, and constantly assure consumers that they can be trusted.

AD: And what would this portend?

CO: It would take on the appearance of "thou doth protest too much." This would cast enormous doubt within our consumer ranks. This would threaten and destabilize the transaction of properties. Consumer doubt or hesitation regarding trust surrounding such an important lifestyle and financial decision would endanger our economy. Not just due to the transactions themselves, but also due to all of the businesses which benefit as a result of a real estate transaction. So this is the first reason why being on and supporting the REALTORS© team is so vital, and a reality that can never be over stressed.

AD: What are some of the other team benefits that perhaps REALTORS© take for granted, or ones that go under appreciated?

CO: Well, the whole notion of marketing properties. Without one major, organized real estate team, that is the National Association of Realtors©, real estate buyers would not enjoy the immense benefit of having access to essentially all of the lifestyle offerings. Also, home sellers would not maximize the laws of supply and demand.

AD: What would the consequence of this lack of access be?

CO: The whole world would become sort of like millions of pocket listings. This would prevent homebuyers from enjoying full choice when deciding upon the right home, the right town, the right school system etc. If NAR did not provide all REALTORS© with the opportunity to come together and create MLS's over the decades, the very nature of lifestyle selection would have been materially injured. Moreover, while everyone talks about the value of the internet and the power of marketing, perhaps our greatest value is through our teamwork, which in a word, is networking. It is the networking dimension of a REALTOR'S© life only made possible through membership within the real estate team, that provides both consumers and REALTORS© the benefits of full transparency and choice.

AD: Charlie, you realize that you are introducing concepts that are already known, so why the passion regarding the importance of our industry's largest and most important team?

CO: Because many REALTORS© do, in fact, take for granted the wonders that the National Association of Realtors© provides its team members. For example, that such organized and vigilantly supported teamwork leads to how team members can caravan at brokers' open houses, and instantly feel welcome and give and receive mutual respect from REALTORS© in all different companies, should never be overlooked as a momentous team oriented ritual. That REALTORS© are able send a referral across the country and never have a second thought that they will be compensated from a closing that they never have to attend, happens simply because they are on the REALTOR© team.

AD: What other benefits of the NAR team would you like to highlight, Charlie?

CO: The National Association of Realtors© provides the greatest volume of relevant real estate related data and information to all of its team members through house logic, and thereby empowers them as trusted advisors. The National Association of Realtors© also provides education from the basics to the most sophisticated and comprehensive levels found through an unending array of classes. These classes and courses are offered off and online, and made available locally and at our conventions. Many of the courses lead to invaluable and leverageable professional designations. These educational opportunities uniquely transcend company affiliation. This is due to the greater form of teamwork which makes it quite natural to learn together as fellow teammates of the larger National Association of Realtors©. Additionally, we actually have competitors sharing business strategies with one another. This all made possible due to how revered and strong the foundation of our primary real estate team is.

Yes, without The NAR team we would not be anywhere near as education or networking evolved. Also, our industry-wide team is involved in numerous community-centric activities such as Habit for Humanity and scores of other community outreach programs. The National Association of Realtors© also provides team members with an amazing array of travel and other vendor service benefits through its members VIP and rewards programs.

AD: Charlie, considering your years as a successful REALTOR© associate, nationally leading manager, co-founder of a major brokerage, past president of the New Jersey Association of Realtors© and VP of the National Association of Realtors©, I want to know the following: If you had to pick the single greatest team benefit of membership in the

National Association of Realtors©, one that also impacts consumers, what would it be?

CO: Allan, without question, professional cooperation and a sense of professional identity together rank highest in my book. I believe that the National Association of Realtors© represents the single greatest example of teamwork of any profession in the world.

AD: How so?

CO: Where else do you have anything quite like how our competitors actually work as collaborators in the marketing and networking of homes for sale? This is one of the great cooperative and teamwork related wonders of the world, that we share, as team members, the home for sale data through MLS and IDX, which incomparably benefits consumers all over the world. The consumer is the ultimate beneficiary of our teamwork. Also, due to NAR efforts the coordination of technology, information, marketing, and networking resources all brings a higher level of sophistication and strategic planning in full view of an increasingly sophisticated consumer. The many benefits of this high level display of forward thinking and overall professionalism accrues to all members of the National Association of Realtors© team. I can think of no professional organization or trade union that has established the level of teamwork that our association has. This undeniable and perhaps under celebrated level of teamwork and the establishment of a united front of coordinated service serves all team members well. Without question, the enthusiastic willingness to professionally collaborate on behalf of consumers and clients is the ultimate display of teamwork. This makes it possible for all companies, real estate teams, and individuals to prosper. The analogy I would use regarding the emphasis of your book is this: just as real estate teams should recognize and be thankful that their broker has established an underlying support system and structure which makes it possible to create a team under its auspices, so too should we never forget of all that we as the National Association of Realtors© team makes possible. People talk about how the Balkanization of countries can hurt one and all – well, because of the National Association of Realtors© sense of teamwork and cooperation, we could be the dictionary example of the words synergy and collaboration.

AD: What would be the biggest losses, was this greatest of all teams ever weakened?

CO: We would not celebrate diversity as we do. We would not participate with real estate professionals throughout the world. We would not have political influence regarding the enormous benefits of home ownership. We would not provide tens of thousands of real estate brokerages the opportunity to remain viable, and instead our industry would consolidate as banks have. We are rapidly seeing a handful of banks taking over essentially the majority of banking in America. I do not want this to ever happen to our industry. Because we all belong to one coordinated professional team, both real estate professionals and consumers are allowed a wide range of choice. Ironically, because our REALTOR© team is "too big to fail" for pure and consumer beneficial reasons, it also keeps any one or handful of real estate companies from ever becoming too big to prevent choice. Also, without our number one industry team the National Association of Realtors©, we would not have committees like our strategic planning committee, which insures that the first major consumer facing real estate website, Realtor.com, bore our team brand. We also would not be able to form the deep and enduring local and international bonds with those members on our National Association of Realtors© team throughout the industry.

AD: Thank you Charlie for reminding Debbie, myself, and all of our readers about the importance of the real estate team that transcends all others.

An Exemplary Edina Realty Team Leader

An interview with Jay Fletch

Allan Dalton: How have you branded your real estate team?

Jay Fletch: As the Jay Fletch Real Estate Group. We abbreviate the name Jay to the letter J, so it is the J. Fletch Real Estate Group.

AD: Why did you select group versus team?

JF: I liked the ring of it better. And I also didn't want it to be Jay Fletch and Associates as there are too many people doing that sort of branding.

AD: How many years have you been in the business?

JF: 19 years.

AD: Which company did you start off with?

JF: I joined Edina Realty in 1997 and I am still there.

AD: That is a tribute to two things: the quality of your loyalty and the quality of Edina Realty. What is the stance of Edina Realty regarding real estate teams?

JF: They are looking very seriously at ways that they can help to further develop and promote real estate teams.

AD: How many offices does Edina Realty have, I know they are legendary, and where did Ron Peltier first became nationally prominent?

JF: Edina Realty, I think has in the neighborhood of 70 offices and about 2,300 agents. We are part of the Home Services Company which is part of Berkshire Hathaway.

AD: How many teams would you say currently exist within Edina Realty?

JF: If I had to guess, I would say about 30.

AD: Which Edina office houses the J. Fletch Real Estate Group?

JF: Woodbury, Minnesota.

AD: How many real estate teams are within the Woodbury Office?

JF: Within the Woodbury Office there are officially two teams. Thus, my definition of a team is where you actually have a team with specific and distinct roles for specific people. Based upon that definition, we have two teams within office here. We have several agents who have an assistant, but I do not think that they would comport to a general description of a team, and I say that with all due respect.

AD: Speaking of Woodbury, how big is the market which your group serves?

JF: We actually serve Washington County in Minnesota and St. Croix County in Wisconsin. We are in a border region so we go back and forth, and then anything outside of this area we refer out.

AD: How many years did you work on your own before beginning your group and why the structural change?

JF: For 17 years I worked as an individual. The reason I made the organizational change, essentially, was for two reasons: time and leverage. A so called tipping point was that I was so consumed with what I was doing, and without team support, that one night I walked out into our office lobby at ten pm, and my daughter was sleeping on the chair. It registered with me in a profound way that I needed to change and fix the way I was approaching my career, my business.

AD: What was the first thing you did to fix the situation you created by being such a dedicated worker that you essentially lost yourself in your work?

JF: Although some people begin the development of their real estate team by first bringing on a buyer agent, I knew what I needed most was an administrative person. The hiring of my first person also reflected my overall philosophy of how a real estate team should function.

AD: How so?

JF: The first thing that an existing top producing agent who begins a team needs to determine is this: What are the $15 an hour tasks, and what are the $100 an hour tasks? Which matters require my specialized attention, and which can be resolved by others? Long story short, for every $15 an hour task that you do not have someone do, and you do instead, you are depriving yourself from doing $100 an hour work. For example, now I have someone who handles all of my marketing and all of my social media. But back then my first hire was for someone to manage my schedule, and I would be lost without her. She now does much more than handle my calls and appointments. She serves as my transaction coordinator and manages all contracts to closing - from inspections to earnest money being received, and all of the processing. And while she is processing all the business I generate, my marketing manager is helping us create the business through her riveting marketing efforts.

AD: What are some of the specific activities of your marketing manager that you value most?

JF: All of my marketing, all of my social media, my happy hours, client parties, and client birthday cards. My marketing manager monitors Facebook to discover the life changing events of my clients and prospects. To me, Facebook would represent a major waste of my time, so I completely ignore it, but she is like my Facebook detective and makes the most of it for me. She is also sending out all my thank you notes and managing my database.

AD: Sounds like your marketing manager is a one person contact management system. Which contact management system does she manage for you?

JF: I have used Top Producer, our company's eConnect, but have recently switched to a CMS that is more geared towards marketing. And I will let you know in the future if they deliver on what they say they do.

AD: As one who used to oversee Top Producer I am pleased to see how contact management vigilant your group is. Who else is on your team?

JF: I have a listing coordinator. This person is basically my listing manager in essence. She manages all listings. She ensures that all our pictures are strategically rotated. She is forensically focused on the appearance of our text regarding all of our properties. This listing coordinator attends all of my closings. Therefore, I do not have to attend them anymore. Allan, last year we had 130 closings. Considering the time it takes to drive there and back and attend the closing from start to finish, that would represent an epic time management disaster for me. Plus, my coordinator has remarkable people skills, is eternally enthusiastic, and everyone loves her. She gives me the confidence that every promise I make to home sellers will be professionally executed. If I promise staging, she makes sure it happens. And my last group or team member is I have one buyer agent. I could have two or more, but I want to maximize the earnings of my buyer agent. Plus, I still will work with certain buyers.

AD: Do you see your group growing or staying relatively small in numbers?

JF: Perhaps if we talk three years from now, we might be double the size, but not if we have to give up on any of the quality we provide my clients. Plus, I see teams with 17 people doing the same production that we are doing with five. Some people want to start teams so they can essentially stop working, yet still have their name on the building. That is not me. These people want to abdicate, I want to delegate. Although I used to work 80 to 90 hours a week, I still work 60 to 65. My goal is to bring on one more team member to get my hours down to 50 a week.

AD: How do your clients respond to how you have structured your team?

JF: Very well, because I not only represent my sellers as sellers, but also as buyers. This way they do not feel that I am giving them the bum's rush, so to speak, by referring them out to a stranger. I expect my buyer agent to work on the leads that my listings generate, and generate their own business, and not to dilute the special bond I create with my home seller clients. Therefore, my marketing, administrative, and listing management group members are all supporting my efforts to market the property, yet my clients largely and consistently are working with me and not being passed on. I am the head surgeon who defines the highest level of professionalism, a level which I consistently provide the vast majority of our seller clients. I would say that 80% to 85% of our sellers are ones I fully represent.

AD: How does your group help you prepare for your listing appointments?

JF: For example, I have a listing appointment today at 4 pm. The listing coordinator will come into my office and she will drop off my marketing pieces, ones that will appeal to this particular seller. She will drop off pictures and profiles of all of the comparable homes to the subject property and the folder will have every conceivable feature and paper work required for me to present and close the listing...bingo. I don't even have to look at it. I just open the folder at 4 pm at the seller's home and am off to the races. I know how my listing coordinator prepares me, and she knows how I like the presentation to be prepared.

AD: When you cite your volume, do you include your buyer agent's business?

JF: My company shows that I did $38 million last year, and the MLS shows $31 million. I only like to take credit for the $31 million that I did and got paid for.

AD: What is your average sales price?

JF: $248,415.

AD: Could you be more specific? Weren't there any pennies involved there? Seriously though, how do you differentiate your group?

JF: First of all, I believe that Edina Realty is the best run real estate company in the country. We have great results to leverage and our brand is second to none in Minnesota. Beyond that, everything I do is to differentiate myself. For example, this is why I hold 14 designations and certifications. So if it is a military family, I hold the certified military professional designation. If I am going after a million dollar listing, I reference my being a certified luxury marketing specialist. If it is a waterfront property, I bring up my resort and second home designations.

AD: Do you compete for listings more against other teams or individual agents?

JF: Still more individuals, but it is changing every year to more teams.

AD: Do you believe the evolution of teams will continue getting more prominent?

JF: Yes, in fact, it seems as though Keller Williams has built their whole organization around the real estate teams movement.

AD: You mentioned possibly adding another team member. What do you want or need the most?

JF: A big time prospector.

AD: What percentage of your business now is from listings?

JF: 70%. Last year we took 146 listings. Shooting from the hip it is probably 70 to 30 in favor of listings, but many of those 30% buyers came from listings. This is why a prospecting member addition appeals to me.

AD: Are you more a leader or manager?

JF: I need to be both. I am not in favor of some team leaders who have 20 or 24 agents now. I see them on team panels, telling everyone what to do to get their business up and going, and this person is completely removed from working with buyers or sellers. I want to both lead my business and also not only mange my group members, but also manage, with the assistance of my staff, the manner by which we directly represent and serve our clients. The other individuals I speak of are running businesses, but not a real estate team or group. This difference concerning being close to the consumer to me is what our business is and needs to be all about.

AD: Do you have aspirations of someday being able to sell your real estate group, and if so, what would be the key to doing so?

JF: By making my group look like McDonald's. And that is what I would mean about not only leading an organization but also managing it. It is critical to have consistency and systems that transcend your leadership and even your brand. This is why a team's database is their single greatest asset. Our database accounts for 80% of our business and why I devote so much time to learning how to best serve others. I probably read 50 to 60 books a year and attend numerous seminars. In fact, I even attended Tony Robbins training in Fiji. I am obsessed with constantly challenging and re-examining all of our team presentations and systems. If you visited my home unannounced, you would see cards and papers posted on walls all over the house on my presentations.

AD: That's amazing, but let me give you this staging tip: when you go to sell, take them down.

JF: Very funny, but what isn't funny is how many Realtors just go through their careers by the seat of their pants.

AD: Do you have an overarching philosophy for your team that has come from all of your reading, family, work, and life experiences?

JF: A few. Always do what's right. Always do more than you are paid to do. And always remain loyal.

AD: Speaking of loyalty, I am sure you are constantly being recruited. It is admirable that you have been so loyal to Edina all these years.

JF: Yeah, like when Keller Williams came into our market and wanted me to be a market center owner. The reason I stay is that Edina is loyal to all of us, is an amazing company synonymous with Minnesota real estate, and how can you ever leave people like Ron and Bob Peltier? Plus, they value education and so do I, which explains my MBA. But of all the things I have ever learned, perhaps the one thought I cherish most is from my favorite author of all time, Jim Rohn, "Don't wish it was easier, wish that you were better." That to me says it all, and is also a major principle of mine; to get better each and every day.

AD: Thank you Jay, for making this book better.

Moving from a Military Team to Leading a Successful Real Estate Team

An interview with Lori Lynn

Debbie De Grote: Let's begin with your beginning in real estate. When did you start?

Lori Lynn: I got my license on Halloween 2002.

DD: Should we read any particular symbolism into that particular date of entry?

LL: I have often wondered, but have not reached any conclusion as yet.

DD: What did you do before entering real estate?

LL: I had earned a bachelor's degree in accounting and I was the controller of our family business.

DD: What type of business was it?

LL: Manufacturing. I was also in the military reserves.

DD: Where did you attend college?

LL: I first went to the University of Wisconsin in Milwaukee and then finished my degree at Franklin College in Columbus, Ohio.

DD: Well, you certainly have deep Midwestern roots, both in terms of education and manufacturing. What category of manufacturing was your family involved in?

LL: My father-in-law was actually the first person to make a plastic drinking straw. Originally the bar straws were always being picked apart so my father-in-law made them out of polythene.

DD: When did he do this?

LL: 1960.

DD: He must have been a remarkable person.

LL: He was amazing and was still inventing things until the day he died at age 92.

DD: What promoted your decision to enter real estate?

LL: Our manufacturing began to suffer due to Chinese manufacturing. Plus, we had a big contract with Dixie straws and when they sold our contract was not honored. Therefore, I decided, even though I was pregnant with our fourth child, to take the classes and get my real estate license.

DD: How did that transition go for you?

LL: My first year, even with another baby being born, I managed to sell 23 homes.

DD: What market was this in?

LL: It was in a suburb of Ohio named Dublin.

DD: How did you start off so strong?

LL: Even though I had lived in Dublin for years, I was originally from Wisconsin where I grew up on a farm. Therefore, I had to find a way to engage more people as fast as possible, and especially homeowners.

DD: So what did you do?

LL: The first thing I did going into Christmas was I bought necklaces from Oriental Trader, little jingle bell necklaces, and I hung them everywhere and passed them out in plastic bags.

AD: Was this was helpful in your success? Your jingle bells system?

LL: Well, I included the note that read: "Jingle Bells, jingle bells, jingle all the way...Lori Lynn is here to tell you: a new career is on the way." I mentioned that I was now in real estate and what I could do for them.

DD: I am impressed that your brain could function well as an accountant, and as a military personal, and yet could move so quickly into a whimsically creative mode. That is so impressive how you opened up and engaged the community that way.

LL: It's funny you say that, because people used to actually say to me after receiving the jingle bells gift, "Lori there is no way you used to be a bean counter."

DD: What a wonderful way to make your transition a fun announcement as opposed to the bland announcement: "So and so just joined the company."

LL: There were 185 homes in our community and my older children and I delivered them along with my tagline: "Moving out or moving in, just call Lori Lynn." For years people would meet me and either say, "My cat still plays with that jingle bell," or "Moving out or moving in, just call Lori Lynn."

DD: Yet, if you're like most top producers or teams you don't use that slogan anymore, right?

LL: Right. I use it a little, but I should start doing campaigns on it like I used to do.

DD: What else did you do to prospect?

LL: Well, I didn't just prospect for sellers. I went to the furniture store where we always bought our furniture from and I told them if anyone is looking for furniture because they may be buying a new house or selling, please put them in touch with me. I would call all the neighbors I knew and would say, "Did you know the neighbors down the street are moving? That made me think about you. Now that you have three children have you ever thought of moving to get more space?" This would often leads to two transactions from these neighbors or friends of mine.

DD: So you contacted them first to announce a recent real estate event in their local area and then naturally transitioned to their potential to buy or sell.

LL: Exactly. I have always been strategic in how I approach my business. It was from my accounting and military background. For example, I would always write down ten people to call each and every time I sat down to use the phone and would not stop until I called ten. The phone was especially important to me because I was never comfortable with knocking on doors. I figured people put in phones to talk to people and they put up doors to keep them away from people, which is why when we walked the neighborhoods with the jingle bell necklaces we just hung them around the mailboxes. I also let everyone know that I was on a mission to drive prices higher in our community.

DD: How hard a worker would you describe yourself to be?

LL: I have always been relentless. I even listed a trailer home in the dead of winter 45 minutes away from my office.

DD: When did you start to build your team?

LL: In 2004. I was entering my third year in the business and was at that time selling 70 houses per year. The first person I hired was an administrative assistant. She was not an agent, just strictly an administrative assistant. I put an ad on Craig's List and found her.

DD: What did she do for you?

LL: She would keep my schedule, put appointments in, do my brochures. I was spending 4% of my income on marketing and about 8% on her. My marketing was always 100% on promoting my properties and not on myself.

DD: How about your farming efforts?

LL: Each year I added another neighborhood, and each one was contagious. Every homeowner received a calendar from my each year.

DD: How many calendars a year do you send out and how successful has this been for you?

LL: I send out 7,500 a year and generate about 15 deals a year from this annual activity.

DD: Do you get more leads from either the calendar or the internet?

LL: They are two completely different lead sources. I get more buyer leads from the internet, but many many more seller leads from my calendars and farming activities. And because my listings generate internet buyer leads, I would say that 90% of my business is off of the web, and I spend a small fortune on web based leads. Plus, the farming based leads are people that already know of me and trust me, so I don't have to do a song and dance to compete for the listing or worry about buyer loyalty.

DD: What was the next step in growing your teams?

LL: Given all of my activity, I hired my first buyer agent in 2005. I used your hiring advice including the use of the DISC. This was 11 years ago and teams were not as prominent in Columbus as they are now. I followed what Keller Williams was saying about how to develop teams as well.

DD: How many buyer agents do you presently have?

LL: I have six.

DD: When you started out you said you were working with many more buyers as a percentage, then when you hired your first buyer agent and administrator that dropped to 50/50. What is your personal percentage now that you have six buyer agents?

LL: I would say about 75% sellers.

DD: Do your buyer agents also list?

LL: I encourage them to do both. I get a tremendous amount of leads in though so their focus is much more on buyers. Because I give them a higher percentage of the commissions than many teams (without revealing what that is) they are expected to pay for their own marketing and administrative costs.

DD: I know that your team name is the Lynn Realty Group. Do you think that by not including your first name that it better features your six colleagues who are part of the group?

LL: Absolutely, that's why I did it. I want them to be so successful and powerful in their own right that I someday never have to work with any buyers. Right now I still have too many buyers who think they need Lori Lynn more than the Lynn Realty Group, and that can only slow our future growth.

DD: How do team members leverage you when they personally go after listings?

LL: Very skillfully. They reference me, my involvement as team leader, my statistics, and often they will have me in to fortify the value of the team member and our team. All they have to do is convince home sellers how they need to go with a team, and once that sale is made, then it clinches the deal because we are the number one real estate team in Dublin, Ohio.

AD: Incidentally, what is the population of Dublin, Ohio?

LL: We are about 75,000. And our average sale price is about $250,000.

DD: How much business did your team do last year?

LL: We sold 237 homes, but only 70 from Dublin itself. We serve six counties.

DD: Let's talk about your people.

LL: Well, my first hire was Sherri, who ironically is my husband's ex-wife. She is the best. She is completely loyal and as honest as the day is long.

DD: Who else did you hire?

LL: I went to our trainer at Keller Williams, whose name is Donna, described the type of person I was looking for, and this led to John who has now been with me seven years. He is absolutely fabulous. Then I hired Eric, and Eric is tremendous in that with his highly successful sales background he is able to not only work buyers but generate listings. Everyone on our team is different, including the two and a half administrators who just work for me.

DD: Do you try to hire people by also keeping in mind geographical territories?

LL: Yes. For example, I hired another great agent named Melinda because of her connections within Hilliard, and she also said she wanted to increase her business by working our Northeast quadrant.

DD: Why did you leave Realty Executives to join Keller Williams?

LL: That's a great story. When I was with Realty Executives I met somebody from Keller Williams and she said, "Hey, why don't come to this class on listings?" And at that point I was more focused on buyers. I went to that class and got eight new listings that week. She then invited me to attend another class. After this class, I was on fire. I liked Realty Executives, they were high quality and treated me great, but the reason I left was when my husband said to me, "When you get involved with these KW people, you become a different person." For me that did it.

DD: How many associates are there in your KW office?

LL: About 300. And that is just in Dublin.

DD: How many of these agents belong to teams?

LL: I would say about 25%. But I predict that ten years from now that number will be double.

DD: How does it benefit your agents and you to be on a team?

LL: A major benefit is that since my agents are competing with all 300 of our agents and 6,000 other agents in Columbus that they are able to leverage all of KW's resources and positioning power, in addition to all of our team's.

DD: Do you retain most of your agents?

LL: Yes, unless they relocate, as two did. And then I had two over the years who remained within Keller Williams.

DD: How pro-teams is KW?

LL: As you know as well as anybody Debbie, 100%, and that is the word out on the street in every market in North America.

DD: Do your team members make more on average than non-team members?

LL: It is not even close.

DD: Why do you think more do not want to work on teams?

LL: We have a lot of people in our industry who have very modest, if any, business backgrounds.

DD: How often do you have team meetings?

LL: Every Tuesday with the complete team including administrative team members we go over everything we are doing. Without this meeting we would not be on target to sell 200 homes this year.

DD: Do you encourage your people to someday start their own team?

LL: Completely. In fact, I have a team member that is preparing to do that as we speak. It's funny, she came to me and was apologizing. I told her that she embodies everything I want my team to represent, individual growth, and how happy I am and proud of her. It's just a winning football team where the head coach is thrilled for his assistant when they move on.

DD: Plus, it is part of your legacy.

LL: I have never been concerned about my legacy when it comes to someone on my team growing. It is all about supporting my team member's legacy.

DD: Thank you for making that point. In a book like this we try to cover a wide swath of ground regarding who different team leaders are and how they think. What you just said about your attitude about a team member to essentially start a competitive team I am sure will be a cause for reflection among many of our readers. Now let me ask you, what do you do to provide training and coaching for you team members?

LL: First of all, Keller Williams is constantly providing outstanding training, including their eight week BOLD training program. And then I have you, Debbie, and Excelleum and the coaching, which to me has been a godsend. Other coaches told me that I needed to treat real estate like a business, but didn't have the business depth I needed. When it comes to business minds, this is one area that I cannot be fooled about. Being coached as an individual is also quite different than being coached as a team leader. An individual agent needs to be coached on their career, a team leader on their business.

DD: How has having a team changed your personal life?

LL: Greatly. It gives me the option of how hard I wish to work, when I want to work, and if I need time off for a family crisis or just plain personal and family time, I can do so. For example, I needed to take time recently to be there for my brother, who was battling cancer. Thank God he is in remission, but my team made it possible for me to take that time off.

DD: I can see why your team would always have your back because of how you express your respect for them and the immense role you are playing in their professional growth. What do you think you provide that they cannot find elsewhere?

LL: Leads, mentoring, office space, care and concern, growth strategies, compassion, friendship. And numerous little things like, since I own a warehouse, they can use that for staging related furniture storage, or the numerous little office supply and marketing costs. All that said, I could never do as much for any of my team as my team collectively does for me. I would be nothing without them.

DD: A great perspective, Lori. Thank you for taking the time to be a part of my book.

An Arizona Real Estate Team on the Move

An interview with Rachael Richards

Debbie De Grote: What is the name of your team, group or association?

Rachael Richards: The Rachael Richards Group.

DD: Which brokerage/brand are you affiliated with?

RR: HomeSmart Select. I am a co-owner with my husband and business partner Ben Quillinan.

DD: How long have you been in the real estate business?

RR: 12 years.

DD: Were you in another career before entering real estate?

RR: I was a flight attendant. My husband Ben and I enjoyed traveling and having fun in our 20s before having children and a career.

DD: At what point in your career did you begin to pay for professional assistance?

RR: Each year my business has consistently grown by 10 to 15%, almost like clockwork. I never had an REO account or any connections with builders. It's just been one client at a time and building a solid foundation which I'm very proud of. When I started real estate, I was still a full-time flight attendant based in New York City and living in Phoenix. I hired a transaction coordinator right away. That first year, I sold 18 homes, which is not bad because I was commuting to New York City from Phoenix. When I was home in Phoenix I focused on generating business 100% of the time. Once I began to sell 40 to 50 homes a year, which was about 3 to 4 years into the business, I hired a full-time assistant. From there, I started building a team. The first focus was an assistant, buyer agents, and then listing agents. I have additional staff members to help support the sales team so they can provide exceptional service and focus on helping buyers or sellers only.

DD: Please walk us through the evolution of your professional support to how you are now structured as a team or group.

RR: It was a very organic process. My strengths are building businesses and developing relationships. Every team member we add allows me to continue to focus on those strengths which ultimately build our organization. I strongly believe in specialization so that we can provide the ultimate service experience. I am very careful when developing a position to be mindful to structure the position so that it is very clear and focused.

DD: When you first decided to brand yourself as a team how was it greeted by your company?

RR: Great.

DD: How was it greeted by your clients?

RR: Most people love the service they get from the team or an organization. It's impossible for one individual to provide the type of service that we deliver. Of course, we have had some growing pains along the way and had to develop systems to support the volume of business that we do. We strive for our clients to feel they are being guided through the process and have clear expectations.

DD: How many teams are now within your company?

RR: We own our brokerage and developed it specifically to house The Rachael Richards Group.

DD: When you compete for listings, is it more likely to be against an individual agent or another real estate team?

RR: I would estimate about 25% are teams.

DD: What do you think your team offers that your associates cannot receive from within any other company?

RR: Our staff and sales agents benefit from an extremely supportive environment. There is a lot of camaraderie and a positive feeling that is difficult to describe. I find that salespeople come to me seeking a position more for the benefits of mentoring versus lead opportunity. Our group is known for the highest work standards within ourselves and for delivering exceptional service. We not only have this reputation within our own industry amongst the agents, we also have a five star reputation within our community. We have been able to generate this reputation through social proof via online reviews.

DD: What is your average sales price and what segment of the market do you work?

RR: The average sale price in our area is about $300,000. Phoenix is a very large marketplace and with a team it is possible to effectively service a larger area than in past years. I am very focused on building a luxury brand within our team.

DD: How often does your team meet?

RR: We meet 30-45 minutes weekly. Recently, we have added 10 to 15 minute huddle meetings once a week. I also invest a great deal of time training newer agents. I spend at least a half an hour with each agent on an individual basis for the first six months. I meet once a month with the listing team and buyer team individually. I utilize technology and voice memos a lot and send out messages to my team on a regular basis. This keeps a connection between us when they are out in the field often.

DD: Are you more of a leader or a manager?

RR: I consider myself more of a leader then a manager. With that being said, it's impossible in my position to not have a combination of the two. I have very high standards for myself and those around me, and I hold them accountable to the same standards.

DD: How has creating a team impacted your personal life?

RR: In some ways it has alleviated a lot of stress, as far as the physical aspect of being out in the field. In other ways it has added a lot of stress because I'm responsible for so much more than when it was just me. It's not as simple and yet, it is worth it and allows me to keep growing and building something that I am very proud of, something that will last longer than it would have if it was just me.

DD: Do you think teams in general provide consumers and clients with better service and value because of a more collaborative approach toward problem resolution? Or less value because the public isn't getting as much attention of the more skilled team leader?

RR: I absolutely feel teams provide better service than an individual agent. In today's world people are extremely busy and demand flexibility. Plus with technology they expect rapid response. We are able to accommodate them because it's more than just me.

DD: How do your team members leverage your professional fame to get listings?

RR: We have standards for service and consistency. Everyone has the same script for buyer or listing presentations, to which they add their own personality.

DD: What percentage of the time do you go on their listing appointments?

RR: I spend most of my time generating business for the organization. The listing agents that I work with are exceptionally skilled at presenting to sellers, and this allows me more time to oversee that our standards are being met and that there's plenty of business coming in the door.

DD: How much total business did your team generate in 2015?

RR: $62 million, 231 units.

DD: How much do you separately brand your team from the company?

RR: Our focus is about the Rachael Richards Group and we utilize HomeSmart to our advantage because of its strong brand name recognition within our area.

DD: Do you use most of the company consumer centric services or create your own?

RR: I do not use our brokerage's marketing. I have developed our own brand.

DD: How has the coaching you have received influenced your team's growth? How do you meet the coaching needs of your associates?

RR: Because I'm in the Black Diamond coaching program with Excelleum, my coaching is overseen by you, Debbie. However, I utilize all the great coaches at Excelleum so I can continue learning from each of them. I love the design and that it is customizable to help not only coach me, but my whole group.

DD: Why should a high producer either stay on your team or join your team versus starting their own?

RR: It's simply impossible for an individual to produce at the same level as an organization. It is also my belief that the high level of standards within a good team will set the bar higher and ultimately you will be more successful because of those around you.

DD: Do you plan on being able to sell your team someday?

RR: Absolutely. I am 43 years old now, and it's definitely not too early to think about things like this. This is why it's so important to develop our group to run with or without me in the day-to-day operations.

DD: Why do you believe that teams have grown exponentially over the past ten years or so?

RR: I believe teams have grown to match the pace of the consumers who demand immediate response and flexibility.

DD: What percentage of your business is made up of listings?

RR: For the last 10 years the business it was about 75% listings 25% buyers. The last two years our buyer team has grown, and last year it was 50/50. We realized a lot of the buyer opportunities we received required more time to nurture. I developed more effective ways for our buyer team to stay in touch with buyers while they are working through their decision-making process. Once we figured that out, the buyer team's productions sky rocketed. Also, we realized they needed less leads to work and added another agent. This year, my focus is on our listing team and building our luxury business.

DD: What percentage of your buyers is a result of the listings you secure?

RR: This is very difficult to measure with internet marketing. 10 years ago a buyer would call on the actual sign, and now the buyer sees a sign, they get on the phone, and inquire through websites such as Zillow or Trulia. At least 50% of buyer business is a result from our listings.

DD: Is there anything else about yourself or your team that you would like to share?

RR: I am extremely passionate about the real estate industry. In my own way, I consider myself a pioneer in developing more innovative and creative ways to work that match with what buyers and sellers want. I've studied a lot about consumers and how crazy busy people are with the demands of work with technology allowing them to be available 24/7. We experience the same within our industry. It's difficult to reach people, let alone get any time with them. Instead of fighting this change I've embraced it and created ways to value our client time. My team and I utilize phone presentations and technology to showcase how we can help them achieve their goals. We make it easy for them, and this is why they hire us!

Are Agents Better Off on Teams or Working Solo?

An interview with Debi Orr

Debbie De Grote: Where is your business located, Debi?

Debi Orr: My home base is Ridgefield. We cover the greater Danbury and northern Fairfield County markets for the most part.

DD: Those are beautiful and classic Connecticut countryside towns aren't they?

DO: Yes, it is a great market to live and work in.

DD: What's the name of your team?

DO: The HomeVision Group.

DD: How did you come up with that name?

DD: It goes back a long time now. In 2002 I teamed up and joined forces with another agent in my former Century 21 office. We both had very active businesses and we did not want either one of our names to represent our team name. We instead wanted a forward thinking name that also spoke to lifestyle. We, therefore, selected HomeVision.

DD: I think the name sounds transcendent.

DO: Exactly, and so did we. That name remains, but our team has totally evolved and changed since we initially formed and branded ourselves.

DD: First of all, which company are you now with?

DO: The company which houses our HomeVision Group is Keller Williams Realty.

DD: Are you the broker?

DO: I am a broker, but not the broker of record of Keller Williams Realty. That would be Rick Scott.

DD: Do you and your partner own the franchise?

DO: Yes we do.

DD: Let me be clear. So you own the Keller Williams local franchise, and within that structure you run a team, which is very typical within Keller Williams.

DO: I have a big foot in each. I have developed a great team where I still do all of the listing side. I have a buyer specialist who handles all buyers, and we have one and a half administrative assistants. One is a marketing and transaction manager assistant while the other is a showing assistant and runner. So I both run my little team and I am also the operating partner of the market center office.

DD: How many associates are within the local KW franchise you own?

DO: We have 95 agents in our Ridgefield/Danbury office. We are becoming larger by the day, as we also, in 2009, invested into the Keller William's Stamford Market Center. My buyer specialist went there and he is now the manager and leader in that office. The way that the Keller Williams model works is the operating partner, which is me, casts the vision for their company and leadership, and holds the person who equates as the manager, but who we refer to as the team leader accountable for growing the market center and helping all KW agents to be as productive as possible.

DD: Who is your partner?

DO: I have a great partner whose name is Rick Scott.

DD: How long did you and Rick have the HomeVision Group at Century 21 before you left and started your KW local franchise?

DO: HomeVision was with us at Century 21 for about a year. We were ahead of our time at Century 21 because they had very few teams in the northeast back then. We moved on to KW right after we learned about them in 2003 at the NAR convention in San Francisco.

DD: And again, how many KW offices were in Connecticut at that time?

DO: We would become the first, which our entire company is quite proud of.

DD: When you started with KW, which brand initially was more important? KW or HomeVision?

DO: Definitely in the beginning it was our HomeVision brand because no one in Connecticut had ever heard of KW. And especially since everyone knew of Century 21.

DD: Of the 95 agents in your company, how many different teams are there?

DO: Three or four if you count husband and wife teams.

DD: Why so few?

DO: A lot of top producers still enjoy going solo. And I completely respect that. I encourage both teams and non-teams. Teams are not for everyone.

DD: How about within that Stamford market center, how many teams are there?

DO: Real estate teams are more prevalent in the much more populated greater Stamford marketplace.

DD: Debi, let's say if a prospective agent came to you as an owner in the company and asked, "Am I better off starting with a team or not joining a team." How would you respond?

DO: Very interesting question. I have two different thoughts about that. First, a prospective agent needs to truly understand the business before they decide on a team because they can miss so much if they limit themselves to a team. Often times an agent in the beginning can learn more from the general company and overall agent population and from the broker. This is especially true if it is a tiny team. This could constrict their growth. On the other hand, if a team is large enough so the educational experience scales, then I would say join that team. What I am saying is that there are a lot of different elements that go into this very important decision.

DD: Yet if you had to say which example yielded the higher average productivity per agent in general, team affiliation or just company or office affiliation, what would it be in your considered opinion?

DO: I would definitely say that productivity per agent would be higher in teams, and fewer agents leaving the business in the first three years. I think the biggest determinant as to whether team members do better and stay in the business has to do with how effective the team is in creating lead generating systems.

DD: Does everyone in your organization have an opportunity to either work within a team or not?

DO: Absolutely, and it isn't just a onetime decision to either join or leave a team, it is a decision that can be made at any time.

DD: Other than a compensation differential, I would think that team members would think they have an advantage because they have all the resources of both the greater company and the team. Would you agree with that?

DO: Generally speaking yes, but again this thinking can be flawed as well, depending upon the circumstances. For example, if someone joins a team and the team is expressly created to support the production and the ego of a team leader who is a listing rain maker, then this leader might prevent certain team members from growing into full service agents who can list and sell, because they are limited to believing they can only excel as a buyer agent.

Or, if one team leader believes that all success depends upon prospecting door to door or cold calling, and isn't up on social media, then this small team and leader can deny certain team members larger exposure to what the rest of the company or industry is doing. On the other hand, someone in the general population of a 50 to 100 person office can absolutely flounder due to not enough activity early on, and get lost in the sauce, as it is very unlikely they will ever get as much mentoring and team support as when on a team. So again, every situation is different.

DD: I can see you have given this a lot of thought. Who has the advantage on a listing presentation?

DO: Again, that depends on how well either type of agent makes their case. A team member can speak to how having the overall resources of both the company and the team, and through collaboration and more intense networking, they have the advantage. On the other hand, a sole working agent can speak to how the home seller might see responsibility diluted through sharing, and raise issues of becoming lost, and how the team might be overly focused on trying to sell their own listings through the small team versus networking more aggressively through the entire company and over all of the real estate community.

DD: If you had to give up either your brand name for your team or the brand name for your company which would it be?

DO: It would be tough, but I place even greater significance on my team's brand. This is also consistent with KW's philosophy though, they teach that we are all more important than any brand.
DD: Do you have an exit strategy for your team?

DO: Yes, here again the importance of the HomeVision Team versus the Debi Orr team, or The Orr and Scott Team. I am more inclined to facilitate someday an evolutionary acquisition where I can leave the business but share in the profits for a period of time. In any event, I am a long way from that.

DD: Thank you Debi.

A Leader Out in Front of Real Estate Teams

An interview with Bob LeFever

Debbie De Grote: Bob, as the CEO of a major Southern California brokerage, Coldwell Banker, going back to 1995 you, as much as any broker in the country, witnessed the evolution of real estate teams. Before we get to how you managed the explosion of teams and groups, tell me a little bit about your early background in real estate.

Bob LeFever: After 5 years in the FBI (and 5 moves) I was looking for stability for my family with two young boys (4 & 2). The real estate broker who sold me my last house kept pursuing me to enter our industry. I did, and with immediate results, becoming a listing machine in a small amount of time. After selling for 2 years, I started my own firm and sold it 3 years later to Merrill Lynch. I eventually became their National Training Director for management and top salespeople. They then moved us to SoCal where I became the general manager of the Beverly Hills Region. This area was their top region in the country the 2 years I was in that position. I then became President of the SoCal company, and then Merrill Lynch was sold to Prudential where I held the same position. Coldwell Banker, in 1995, recruited me to the position of President for their Southern California region. From there I started my consulting and coaching career.

DD: So, in a sense Bob, although it would be a stretch, you were the team leader of quite a major real estate operation. How much volume did the company do?

BL: I oversaw 100 offices with 5,000 salespeople. Our sales volume was $22 billion with a gross revenue of $550 million.

DD: How did you see the company change during that time?

BL: I spearheaded 22 acquisitions over a five year period. The two largest being the Jon Douglas Company and Fred Sands Realty. These two companies added 2,000 salespeople to our sales organization. The key for our success in converting these companies to our culture was to guide them to look at what we just created and look to the future. It was an amazing success. These companies were icons in the industry and known nationally. Our parent company was nervous with these acquisitions because our senior management team was from the East Coast. Marketing was totally different on the West Coast. Also, the concept of teams was becoming a common occurrence, but not so much on the East Coast. Embracing the team culture was paramount in keeping everyone excited about these mergers. My senior management team did an outstanding job in having these newly acquired agents understand that we had just created the third largest real estate company in the world.

DD: So let's move on to the evolution of teams in Southern California, specifically to your company.

BL: Teams originally were husband and wife teams or teams made up of family members. But then in the mid-90s top producers started to understand that they could do more volume and increase their income significantly with administrative help and the concept of buyer agents. Some of these succeeded, but many struggled because the top producer (team leader) was not trained or equipped to manage this process of hiring the right person, understanding the details and implementation of a job description, and managing people day to day. Commission schedules were a challenge for the broker because many top producers demanded the commission from the buyer agent be paid to the top producer at their high split and then the team leader would pay a portion of that to the buyer agent. Today this is still a challenge for the industry. The models for this commission distribution vary all over the country.

DD: Bob, you mentioned different forms of teams. Give me some more detail.

BL: During my CEO tenure I experienced teams being simply two people to teams with dozens of members. The consumer embraced the team concept more easily than the industry did. When teams grew in number, the natural conflict for the broker was office space for both team administrative staff and buyer agents. Conferences with team leaders always centered around what was profitable for them and what was profitable for the company. This was also true of commission splits. There had to be an understanding that the company was there to make a profit and would help the team leader also be profitable. That discussion still exists today.

DD: How did your 100 managers react to the growth of teams in their new offices?

BL: Branch managers were paid on the bottom line and had a natural dislike for teams. In offices where rent was very high, the manager demanded that the team participate in the expense of the rent. Also, branch managers were opposed to the idea that the team leader (e.g. 80% split) received the commission on each transaction of all team members (e.g. 60% split). Another important conflict developed where branch managers also demanded that each agent on a team pay E & O premiums. Initially, team leaders only wanted one premium for the entire team. Many of these conflicts have now been resolved, and today many of the top offices in the country have several teams working within them.

DD: How did you integrate these team cultures within your overall company culture?

BL: Rather than focus on the 1990s, let me address what we see today. Today we see teams operate in all company cultures. Some cultures have embraced the team concept totally, and actually have training for the team leaders and the agents within them. Less than 15 years ago all brands at their conventions had no awards for teams and that certainly has changed today. Even the *Wall Street Journal* publishes the top teams in America. The coaching is both for the leader and all team members, including the administrative staff. Team leaders lean on us heavily for the selection process, job descriptions, the training process, and managing the group in general.

DD: Do you think the real estate downturn further contributed to the evolution of teams?

BL: The REO business fueled the evolution of the first teams being of a larger scale. The family team I remember best was Victor and Elizabeth Leon, the husband and wife who were consistently one of the top husband and wife teams in the greater Los Angeles area. They specialized in the REO market in the higher end properties. Victor was the prospector, calling on banks, and Elizabeth was in the office making sure all the details were taken care of in a very demanding aspect of our industry. A perfect marriage so to speak! The most productive team for Coldwell Banker year after year is the Joyce Essex team. Joyce and her husband Harvey have put together a phenomenal administrative team. To be in their office is like watching an orchestra perform. Everyone has a defined role.

DD: Were you able to downstream your company's ancillary services through the teams' within the company's organization?

BL: Yes, our culture was supplying ancillary services around the real estate transaction. We were simply doing what every industry does. You don't see branch managers financing their cars through BMW credit. This is common sense. Teams supply much better service to their clients if all the services are done by trusted individuals. Obviously there are RESPA guidelines that must be met. Some of the top teams in North America have established sound relationships with mortgage, title, and closing service companies to a strong mutual benefit.

DD: Bob, what percentage of real estate teams in North America do you believe have committed to coaching contracts?

BL: Essentially, all the top teams are under coaching and some have multiple coaches. There is a culture for each team that is established during the coaching; very carefully making sure that each team member understands the mission of the team leader. Also, job descriptions are prepared so each member clearly understands their role and what is expected of them. Some leaders want their individual team members to be coached individually as part of their Excelleum coaching program. I personally have worked with some of these teams, and it is exciting to see the results when everyone understands their role and what is expected of them. This is especially true of the administrative staff. This selection process of key admin people is the key to a team being successful, and essential for the time management of the team leader. This is why we rely so heavily on the DISC analysis in the recruiting of the key admin person. It must be the right fit. Remember, opposites attract. The team leader does not need a clone, he or she needs someone to keep them organized with their own business and yet, help in managing the team, reflecting the leader's desires and goals. We coach these admin people also. They truly make a team function properly.

DD: Bob, what advice do you give when you're coaching real estate teams about selling their business?

BL: Selling a team, like any business, is a complicated process. Having spearheaded 22 acquisitions and mergers I can tell you with experience that when someone purchases a real estate business they are not buying physical assets or an inventory as in the sale of an ordinary business. They are purchasing the team members who are all independent contractors who can walk out if they don't feel enamored with the purchaser. The team leader has to carefully seek legal advice and turn to financial experts to put together the purchase agreement. Many questions need to be asked such as, is this a cash purchase, stock purchase, installment purchase, does the team leader stay, does their name stay, etc. This is a very complicated transaction!

DD: Bob, you have excelled brokerages both on the east and the west coast. Is there any difference when it comes to teams?

BL: There are differences and they are acute. Specifically, the east coast for most of the last 40 years has been a broker-centered culture. Whereas the west coast, and specifically California, evolved more as an agent-centered culture. Therefore, it was only natural that real estate teams would form earlier and with more resolve on the west coast than the east coast. That said, over the past several years, we're witnessing a balancing out not only between the east and the west coasts, but the entire country, so that teams are now commonplace in all 50 states and Canada. Today there is no difference between the two coasts. Team leaders have reached out to other team leaders at brand conventions and other meetings to learn from each other. Some of the most productive teams can be found in Manhattan, Los Angeles, Chicago, Seattle, Boston . . . you get the idea. Teams are a national movement and will continue to grow.

DD: Bob, you mention you had 100 managers. Which of your managers best made the conversion from office manager to team leader, and who are they?

BL: One would be Peter Hernandez, managing partner at Teles Properties, with 550 agents and 80 teams. The other is Scott MacDonald, managing a large branch in a high end community on the west coast for Berkshire Hathaway.

DD: Why these two out of the other 98?

BL: Peter's company has totally embraced the team concept. They have training for team leaders and team members and all the documentation to set up a team is prepared for the team leader. But more than anything is Peter's amazing dedication to all things coaching, and an example of this goes back to 20 years ago when he was one of my managers. His answering machine voice message was, "I'm busy coaching one of my agents, I'll get back to you." Now regarding Scott, he happens to have one of the largest teams in America in his office. Scott stated to me, "We would have our heads buried in the sand if we did not understand that the consumer has totally embraced the team concept in real estate."

DD: Before joining the real estate industry you spent years, Bob, on another quite famous team. Tell us about that experience.

BL: Debbie, you're right. While I had played sports at the university level and coached after graduating, I had never seen the principals of teamwork, including in real estate and my years in consulting to Fortune 500 companies, that even remotely compares to the esprit de corps and components of teamwork as I did within the FBI. Most memorable was the clear distinction that was obvious to all FBI teammates. We were the good guys and the criminals were the bad guys. The teams that I coach, the ones that enjoy the greatest success, also form around that basis. Their team is righteous and high minded and exceptional. And while their competition does not represent the bad guys, they are their competitors. That's just a fact of life. Let me speak to how teamwork is created in the FBI. First, let me mention that on a yearly basis thousands of individuals apply to be FBI agents but only 800 or so are selected. The training is 16 weeks and quite intense. Our class started with 55 and only 42 graduated. You will be surprised to learn that FBI offices are divided into teams. Most offices will have several teams, all specializing in different areas of the law, such as theft, kidnappings, national security, bank robberies and burglaries, terrorism, espionage, etc. Each team had a supervisor (the team leader). I had some harrowing experiences in some of these areas. There was no misunderstanding by anyone what their role was. Every step was carried out with precision. This life experience was the ultimate team experience.

Legendary Educator Leading a Long and Foster Team

An interview with Gee Dunsten

Allan Dalton: You are the only person I know who ran a small but productive real estate team, while also serving as President of the National Association of REALTORS® Council of Residential Specialists. How did you manage to do both?

Gee Dunsten: Allan, for the past 30 years I have averaged over 120 days a year on the road as a CRS/real estate instructor. The only way I've been able to do this is by forming my own small real estate team over 30 years ago.

AD: You were ahead of your time, Gee. How many transactions would you say that you and your team have produced over that time span?

GD: Well over 2,500 transactions.

AD: And what is the size of your team?

GD: The Dunsten Team is essentially a constant team of three, with one additional position being consistently a temporary position.

AD: Describe the structure, Gee.

GD: Well, I am the team leader and I have a partner, Mark Glushakow, and an administrative maestro, Terry Carey. Mark handles everything for me when I am on the road, just as I would if I were there, and also lists and sells himself. Terry is essentially the right hand person for both Mark and myself and the hub of the wheel. Terry not only handles every conceivable administrative and communication function that my brokerage requires, she also completely manages my travel and educational and coaching schedules.

AD: You mentioned a temporary person. What role do they play?

GD: The way our team seems to function year after year is that we usually have a third person on the sales and marketing brokerage team who performs dozens of client-related, prospecting, marketing, and servicing tasks that require a real estate license. Typically, when this person gets busy and proficient enough to run their own business, they leave to go on their own.

AD: Why don't they stay on The Dunsten Team?

GD: Because they see great value in being trained in our system to be an individual personal producer. Since becoming a partner is not an option, when they reach that point and they are ready to fly, we encourage and support them. We then enjoy a shared mutual respect throughout our careers.

AD: I still don't completely grasp why they cannot do that within your team.

GD: You are right, Allan, but let me just say that Mark, Terry and I are completely comfortable with how our three-person entity functions. We have turned down numerous requests to join us from other agents, because we are not looking to build a bigger, *busier*, and more profitable team. We prefer a small, perhaps busier to a degree team, and only more profitable if the profit never comes at the expense of how we choose to operate.

AD: Can you explain further please?

GD: Allan, I have taught courses in all 50 states and spoken at numerous conventions for almost 40 years. I have seen countless numbers of brokers, teams, and individual agents spend a career steeped in stress because they were always chasing someone else's definition of success.

AD: And what is your definition of success, Gee?

GD: For me, success is making enough money to live comfortably, and to do so without introducing unnecessary stress.

AD: How are you able to do this?

GD: By dividing my time between being on the road teaching and sharing what I've learned over decades in real estate, and staying active in the industry with my team when I return. I can't stress enough the importance of having a team I can count on to hold down the fort while I'm away. This way I'm not stressed out while on the road worrying about what's going on back in the office, and when I return I'm not dealing with the personal problems and dynamics that tend to multiply with each individual participant on the team.

In fact, Allan, this team model is precisely what allows me to utilize my 40 years of experience in the industry as an educator, author, top-producer, and now, thanks to Debbie, Excelleum coach, and share that with our clients.

AD: So what I'm hearing is that the way you want to live and work is even more important to you than how much money you make.

GD: That is precisely what I'm saying.

AD: You must be very organized to manage a real estate brokerage, national speaking, and coaching. Can you please speak to how you and your team of basically two producers create the number of transactions that you do?

GD: It's all about teaming with the community and making the community a part of your real estate team.

AD: Can you give me some examples?

GD: Well, one thing I've learned from all the classes I've taught and the tens of thousands of agents I've spoken to across the country, is that it's all about creating visibility within your community, and visibility as a trusted real estate advisor. That is the emphasis of my team.

AD: How do you do this?

GD: Currently, I am utilizing three community differentiators. First, I created a customized website about my primary market, Ocean City, MD, which has received rave reviews. Second, I also created a world-class video about Ocean City, which you can see by visiting my website or going to Ocean City Gee Dunsten. Third, I use the program which you, Debbie, and Pete Mitchell created as part of the Community Customized Marketing System, called "Neighbors Know Best."

AD: Please tell us about that program, Gee.

GD: "Neighbors Know Best" is a direct mail, email, social media, and postcard branded campaign that asks the neighbors of all The Dunsten Team listings to write testimonials and resident reviews of their neighbor's home.

AD: I see. While most of our readers do not travel half the year, the importance of this interview is to show that if someone who does travel that much can still manage to do more than 100 transactions a year, there is a lot to be said for strategizing, organizing, delegating, community marketing, educating, coaching, and teaching. One last question: I'm assuming that traveling as you do, you are not married?

GD: Actually, I've been happily married to the same wonderful woman for 47 years. We have raised five children and are now enjoying our five grandchildren. To give credit where credit is due, I should say that although my wife, Susan, is an unofficial part of my team, there is no way I could do what I do without her love, support, encouragement, and guidance.

AD: How could Debbie and I not have someone who accomplishes all that you do for the industry, with and beyond your team in the book? Thank you, Gee.

Leveraging Technology to Build a Team of Teams

An interview with Rachelle Willhite

Debbie De Grote: Rachelle, what is your team name?

Rachelle Willhite: Best Choice Realty.

DD: So you have a team that is not immediately defined that way.

RW: That's right, we function completely as a team, but our name suggests full service real estate. I am, therefore, the owner of a real estate company that, in essence, is a real estate team.

DD: That's great, as this book will celebrate many distinctive compositions of teams. The value of your story, I suspect, is that it will help to encourage some people who want to start their own team to do it within their own company.

RW: You got it. That's me, or rather that is us.

DD: How long have you been in business?

RW: Since 2012.

DD: But I am sure you have been in the real estate business for longer than four years, right?

RW: Yes Debbie, I have been in the real estate business as a designated broker working for my own company, as well as another company that was a franchise, for 16 years now.

DD: That still only represents a relatively short period of time.

RW: Debbie, like you, I entered real estate very early. I actually bought my first home with my dad when I was 17, and we began fixing and flipping homes. Then, when I was in college, I decided to get my real estate license and join a firm. I caught the real estate bug I guess you could say.

DD: Okay, please take me through the decision making path that you followed to first join a real estate company, and then deciding to start your own company and structure it as one team.

RW: Well, I was working for a large national real estate company, helping them grow their business by managing and opening offices across the country. The markets were quite diverse, as in Salt Lake City and Philadelphia. This experience taught me that there were opportunities regarding how to build a solid team culture. Therefore, I took the opportunity to move back to Seattle with the vision of creating a real estate team culture. I found out early on that there was resistance with the company I joined regarding my growing a real estate team within their conventional walls. Therefore, I began interviewing other real estate companies, including Keller Williams. Even before KW began to go all in regarding supporting teams, I was already building my real estate team. I was a team leader, more than just being a broker who supported a team. I, instead, was a broker who ran a team.

DD: How did you grow?

RW: Due to my local market knowledge, reputation, and passion for recruiting truly professional teammates, I have been able to grow my real estate team from about 20 agents in 2014 to where our team now, which consists of more than 150 team members.

DD: Let me make sure that I am following your career path. You started flipping homes with your dad then got your license in college and joined a brokerage. Then somebody latched onto your considerable leadership, management, and marketing skills and you became part of a national real estate franchise, then you came back to Seattle, started with one non-team supportive company and then started your own brokerage, which was completely based upon real estate team principles. Is this a correct rendering of your path? And who was the national franchise?

RW: Those are the highlights, and the brand was Zip Realty.

DD: I am going to put you on the spot now Rachelle, what were the opportunities being missed at Zip?

RW: Agent compensation and management to agent communication. Most damaging was that members of Zip teams were, in my view, not adequately informed regarding how they were being compensated. Fair compensation is supremely important to me. Another missed opportunity had to do with training. This is why I later connected with you, Debbie. I was in the middle of my development of training with this company, and I recognized the need for your coaching and your skillset for coaching others. Especially how you not only coach team leaders, but your specialty being coaching entire real estate teams, and with the interests of each real estate team's culture in mind. Debbie, as you know, we pride ourselves on having an elite team of accomplished professionals, and they love how they have access to your varied faculty of great coaches and career strategists.

DD: Thank you Rachelle. I love your brand because it represents the Best Choice for both consumers and agents.

RW: Exactly and thank you for reaffirming this.

DD: How many agents are in your elite group?

RW: Of my 160 agents, 15 have evolved their careers to elite group status, and as you know, these 15 receive specialized coaching from Excelleum.

DD: Now, these individuals not only belong to the mega team, the Best Choice team, but also they have created individual subsets, or teams of their own.

RW: That's right. We have, as an example, the Charlene Little Group, the Deanna Fulton Homes Group, and the Larry Littrell Team. What's also important to focus on is how in Washington State there is a big trend to have very independent brokers and brokerages. They are all independent contractors within a brokerage, but they license themselves either as sole proprietors or as an LLC. We are licensing all of our independent contractors in the same fashion, but they can all operate their own small business. They also have the benefit of working for a company or firm.

DD: How many distinct teams do you have within your company?

RW: Each of our agents has to have their license, whether it be just their name or they have a team under them, and we have about 40 who lead teams.

DD: So perhaps the best description of your culture is that Best Choice Realty is a team of teams.

RW: You nailed it Debbie.

DD: How often does the company come together for events or training where everyone is invited and involved?

RW: Because our teams and their members are all so busy, I prefer, as do they, that we meet more virtually than aggregating physically in person as one big group.

DD: And how often is that?

RW: Every Monday night for the last two years I have conducted a 30 minute virtual conference for everyone. I use the information I get from coaching with you, and then repurpose it and personalize it for my company and our market.

DD: Where else do you meet?

RW: Once a month we meet with groups in one of our offices. These, however, are brain share meetings, and not lectures. We also host larger semiannual events each year. We have the Best Choice Realty anniversary event in the spring, where we invite our agents to a venue to learn from a distinguished speaker and to celebrate another spectacular year at Best Choice Realty.

DD: So you, as the founder and leader, are constantly involved in the career development of everyone?

RW: Yes. As the founder and leader I know that my greatest responsibility is to support the growth of everyone on our entire team.

DD: Rachelle, how much of your time is devoted to personal brokerage?

RW: I spend very little time on personal brokerage, and essentially only serve the needs of family, friends, and neighbors who would be offended if I did not help them. The rest of my time, which is the vast majority, is devoted to team growth. I would say this is about 90% of my time.

DD: Well, since you are technically the broker, let me ask you a question that concerns many of our broker clients. Specifically, how do you react to teams that want to basically obscure the company brand?

RW: This depends upon what you mean by obscuring our company brand. I would say that out of our 40 teams, there are only one or two teams that change our colors. These few exceptions however, are teams with exceptional success and who support everything else about our overall culture. The other teams, many of which also experience exceptional success, recognize the value of overall brand consistency, and seek to differentiate themselves along different lines.

DD: Do you coach your teams on how to lead their teams?

RW: Absolutely, yes. Both through formal training and my open door policy, I am constantly working with team leaders in some way.

DD: Have you been successful in acquiring or outright recruiting other entire teams?

RW: Yes, and will do this much more. Debbie, you have helped us with this.

DD: How do you think the competitors in Washington view your company of teams?

RW: As the most progressive and nimble real estate company in the state.

DD: What is your company's compensation model?

RW: Our structure is the flat fee model for a transaction. Our agents can chose to split their transaction commission with their team members in the way they choose.

DD: What general and administrative services does corporate perform downstream to the teams?

RW: We have two positions that we allow each team to utilize. One is a marketing coordinator and the other is a licensed transaction coordinator.

DD: Do you provide consistent marketing materials to all teams?

RW: We have created templates and listing and buyer presentation packets. The teams then have the option to build these programs out and private label to their teams.

DD: So you have companywide branded programs that each team can customize?

RW: Yes and, of course, they pay for this.

DD: Would you say that your company of teams is more successful at attracting either buyers or sellers?

RW: We record those numbers. In our first year of business, as a team, we were all working with more buyers than sellers. Yet, in the past 12 to 18 months more of our business is listings. Debbie, you and your company are instrumental in this shift.

DD: How much dedication do you devote to your company website?

RW: I have a strong tech background going back to my Zip Realty days. My husband designed our website utilizing third party systems and, of course, partnering with IDX. Each member of our company receives individual mentoring from our tech mentoring program.

DD: It sounds like you also work as a husband and wife team, is that a fair assessment?

RW: Absolutely, my husband is our IT director who works full time and is invaluable.

DD: What do you do within the industry to reinforce your thought leadership?

RW: I am very active in our NWMLS. I was recently nominated to run for one of our open board positions, and will let you know the outcome. That said, my greatest concern is serving my teams and how they serve their clients.

DD: How concerned are you regarding issues of agent retention?

RW: While we budget for attrition, we see very little, and do not see it as an issue. This is not because we take our teams and their agents for granted. Instead, it is precisely the opposite. We do not have an attrition problem like many other companies because we don't take our teams for granted. Instead, we work each day to honor them and our relationships.

DD: What type of agents best fit your culture?

RW: Folks who already owned a business, as they typically are more entrepreneurial and already have online and offline followings.

DD: What did you take from Zip Realty and what did you learn from interviewing with KW that might have shaped your team related vision?

RW: The Zip Realty piece of technology is the obvious answer.

DD: Are there any other questions that you believe I can ask that would reveal more about your team of teams culture?

RW: Let me answer my own question as a way of summarizing the important points that we may have left out. First, I want to grow to 200 team members. I believe the key to my success is the combination of autonomy and strenuous guidance I provide to all our teams. The company is not about my ego, which is why it does not bear my name even though I run the company. My husband helps me, as does my 20 year old sister who is a world class administrative assistant. Also, I do not spend time trying to compare our company to others. I always show respect to competitors and believe our clients must always come first. In a nutshell, I am an efficiency expert. For my team development I believe in technological driven efficiencies, more efficient use of brick and mortar, and in the empowerment of others. Where I see the future of our team is linked to your coaching Debbie, specifically because I spent time in a buyer side lead generational culture that was Zip Realty, where I developed more proficiency and programs to attract buyers. Now, on the contrary, our future, with your help, will be in helping my teams to dramatically accelerate their ability to also attract more home sellers.

DD: Thank you Rachelle, for the privilege of learning your personal journey to becoming a company.

My Team Enabled Me
to Retire Early

An interview with Roddy McCaskill

Allan Dalton: Roddy, let's start with, when did you enter the real estate business?

Roddy McCaskill: I started in real estate 40 years ago and started my team 16 years ago.

AD: I assume you started out as a single agent working with a real estate company other than your own.

RM: Yes, I started out with a man named Patrick Harding.

AD: Did you start your team there?

RM: No, I first worked for a few real estate companies, and then I decided to go into business for myself. So I started up what I guess you would call a traditional real estate company, which I ran that way for about seven or eight years.

AD: When you say traditional real estate company, how do you mean that? How would you define that?

RM: Well, the way I would define it is that we were established basically the same way probably every other real estate company I knew was set up. We had a broker, who was me, an office administrator, and then I had six or seven independent agents who split their fees with me.

AD: Were you part of a franchise?

RM: No.

AD: Where and when did you go from running a so-called conventional real estate company into a different real estate structure?

RM: It began when I closed my company, joined a larger real estate company, and started to build a team there.

AD: What was the name of that company?

RM: Adkins, McNeil, and Smith.

AD: And how long did you stay with them?

RM: For about five years.

AD: When you started building your team at that company, how many other companies had teams in your market?

RM: Not a one, it was unheard of!

AD: And your marketplace was?

RM: Central Arkansas.

AD: What motivated you to start a team?

RM: I was following a real estate educator by the name of Howard Brinton.

AD: I knew Howard well, and respected him, as all who knew him, immensely.

RM: Amen. I went to Howard's seminar. The first one my wife and I went to was for couples who were in real estate. It was in Aspen, Colorado in the early 1990s, and there I met with other top producers who showed me how they had started teams. They told me that it was the best way to be in business, and it was where the industry was headed, for the best business people that is.

AD: How did you start changing your business because of this great exposure through Howard Brinton and the teams he had been working with?

RM: Well, my wife became my head of administration and then I hired a buyer agent. Shortly thereafter, I hired another full time buyer agent. Because of my two buyer specialists, I was now free to generate a lot more listings, which meant we were overwhelming the rest of the company.

AD: Was this viewed as a positive or a negative for the broker?

RM: They were broker partners and they were flipping out.

AD: I'm sure when you say they were flipping out you don't mean they were flipping real estate.

RM: If there's any confusion, let me just say they were freaking out. The reason being my team was so busy and doing so much production that we were dominating the copy machine and the phone lines. Therefore, I decided to start my own company again, but to run it 100% as a team. I had gone the other route of running a conventional company and did not want that again.

AD: What is the difference?

RM: Well, there are many types of teams, husband and wife, mother and son, father and daughter, etc. And then there are teams where everyone is the same and they all go out to get listings and buyers. I decided and made it clear that my real estate company would work as a team that was devoted to completely helping me do more business. In return, they all knew that they would be generously and fairly compensated for their dedication to the team and specifically the team leader.

AD: What was the name of your new company?

RM: Roddy McCaskill Realty, but it functioned completely as The Roddy McCaskill Team. I was not the least bit interested in pretending I was running a democratic real estate office or company, instead it was all about the Roddy McCaskill team but was legally set up with a DBA for a company.

AD: How many people were a part of Roddy McCaskill Realty?

RM: 10.

AD: At your height of doing business, how many members of the Roddy McCaskill Team took listings?

RM: Only me when it came to securing listings. Roddy was on first, second, third, and home plate - that was the game.

AD: I love the baseball metaphor. And how much volume did your team do in a market where the average sales price was what?

RM: About $50 million with an average sales price of about $200,000.

AD: I love your creativity, because how many of the teams that you first met through Howard Brinton were doing it the way you were?
RM: Absolutely none. They were from bigger markets, bigger companies, and they were all creating teams that they called companies within a company.

AD: But it sounds like when you tried it that way originally that the greater company was being swallowed up by your bigger fish.

RM: Exactly. You see Allan, we don't have real estate offices with 50 to 150 agents, where there are a dozen to 100 branch offices, and where a small team can comfortably fit within these mega offices and companies.

AD: This is why Debbie De Grote wanted me to interview you, Roddy, as a blueprint for the many smaller markets. That is, where a rainmaking listing agent might be better off not trying to be a team within a small company, and not starting their own small company, but starting a team as a small company. Speaking of Debbie, what role did Debbie play in your growth?

RM: An enormous role. She coached me on how to recruit, develop people, run my business, and get listings.

AD: Our readers are definitely going to want to know, who were the other nine people that you hired?

RM: A listing manager, a closings manager, and seven people who either just handled showings or were buyer agents. This way I never had to take my time showing property, and instead could prospect, market, and network for listings full time.

AD: So you basically were a Central Arkansas listing machine, one that was smart enough to give the home sellers and buyers the comfort that they were dealing with a real estate company. Yet, you also seemed to meticulously manage the behavior and expectations of your team associates by defining for them that the Roddy McCaskill Team was also blessed in having a king, and you, in fact, were that king.

RM: Since you put it that way, that sums it up nicely and I like the ring to that. That said, I loved my team and treated them that way. I would never take buyers from them, even if it was an $800,000 buyer with one day to buy. No sir, I always treated everyone by the Golden Rule. My wife treated everyone Golden too. She always made sure that all I ever had to do was focus on listings. She handled all administrative worries for me.

AD: What was the number one method you used to secure listings?

RM: It was what I call smiling and dialing. I had a 3-minute timer on my desk I used for years to make sure I didn't spend too much time on any one call. Yes sir, I kept smiling and dialing.

AD: Sounds like a show on TV when I was a kid, dialing for dollars. And by the way, you have a great phone voice.

RM: Well, I have always been told that, and that I relax people on the phone, which is important.

AD: Speaking of relaxing, what is retirement like? Did you sell your company? And do you miss the business?

RM: I do not miss one thing about the business and love our retirement. We live on a lake about 30 minutes away. And I must say that the major reason I was able to retire as early as I did, and as comfortably as we are, is because of my real estate team. This is also because I arranged for one of my buyer agents to take over my team.

AD: I want to end by saying I love how your high intelligence made you one of the first people in our industry to start a company as a team, and how you looked out from your somewhat small and remote marketplace to learn from the Debbie De Grotes and Howard Brintons of the world. Then in return you taught as much, if not more, than you learned.

RM: Thank you Allan, and give my best to all the real estate team leaders out there.

A Business Owning Past, Crucial to a Team Future

An interview with David Lawson

Debbie De Grote: When and why did you enter the real estate business?

David Lawson: I started right out of college in 1978 and went into full-time selling of real estate in 2000. I owned and operated several other real estate related businesses and it was the thing I was most passionate about.

DD: What did you do before real estate?

DL: I owned a real estate management company, a real estate investment company, and an escrow company, along with several other businesses including a trucking company, entertainment ticket sales, a limousine company, a manufacturing company, a coaching and consulting company, and I was also an owner/driver of a NASCAR stock car racing team.

DD: Wow! How did all these career pursuits influence what you have done in real estate?

DL: All of my prior businesses helped me tremendously in my real estate business, especially the real estate related businesses. Selling real estate is a business, not a hobby.

DD: Talk about your early years, which company you began with and what you did originally to set your path towards success.

DL: Once I decided to go into full-time real estate selling, I joined Rocky Mountain and Associates, the oldest real estate company in Park City, Utah. In the very beginning, I built my business on prospecting, lead follow-up, and following my schedule.

DD: What geographical market did you serve then and now?

DL: Park City, Utah and the outlying areas.

DD: Did you segment any particular market?

DL: Early on in my real estate career in Park City, I focused on the area around the Canyons ski resort. In addition, I worked expired listings and FSBOs.

DD: What percentage of your business in the early years was from listings versus sales?

DL: My business started out 81% listings, 19% buyers.

DD: When did you begin to add service staff to your personal operation?

DL: I hired my first assistant in the first year and my first buyer agent in the second year I was in the business.

DD: When did you officially become a team and what name did you select for it?

DL: 2002, and I called it The Lawson Real Estate Team.

DD: So, as you said, the first position you hired was an assistant. What did this person do for you?

DL: She was essentially my listing coordinator and my closing coordinator. She handled everything for me in the business that did not include what I consider to be income producing activities. My job is to prospect, do lead follow-up, go on listing appointments, set up buyer appointments with my agents, and negotiate contracts.

DD: How many other teams were there at Rocky Mountain and Associates, and was there any resistance to your becoming a team?

DL: There were not any other teams in the company or really any teams in Park City, we were the first one. I got a lot of resistance from a lot of people, but I knew it was the only way for me to grow my business the way I wanted.

DD: When there is resistance from brokers and company owners, what do you believe causes it?

DL: For the last five years or so, I was with a different brokerage and they made it difficult for our team to operate. I believe the reason some brokerages don't like teams is that they want agents to promote their brokerage and not the individual team.

DD: Getting back to the development of your team, take me through its growth in terms of personnel including what function each team member serves.

DL: First was the assistant, second was the buyer agent. My next hire was a closing coordinator and then another agent that did listings and helped with buyers. After this I hired an office manager and then a low cost, part-time person to help the team with running errands and organizing all of my prospecting. Next came a marketing person and a couple more buyer agents that also do listings.

DD: Do you consider yourself more of a team leader, team manager, or both?

DL: My team has grown to ten people and now I am not really the team leader, as I have hired a team manager/operations manager. We make decisions together on what we want to do but I have given them full authority to manage the day to day operations.

DD: Is the function of your team that team members are hired and compensated to support your efforts, or does the team exist to equally support the efforts of all team members or both?

DL: All team members work to support each other and the efforts of everyone.

DD: How do you differentiate your team value from the greater brokerage value of the host company?

DL: We do so many things differently than the general brokerage community and we are constantly trying to differentiate what we do as a team versus what the agents do on their own. I believe a large reason for our success is how we differentiate ourselves from others.

DD: How much of your time is devoted to personally working with sellers versus buyers?

DL: I focus most of my time working on getting listings and working with sellers. When I find a buyer, I turn them all over to my buyer agents.

DD: Do you have team members who both list and sell?

DL: Yes.

DD: Do you assign your team members geographical farms?

DL: Yes and no. We do have agents that are more familiar with particular geographical areas in our marketplace and we try to give those agents the clients that are interested in these areas.

DD: How often does your team meet? And can you describe a typical team meeting?

DL: The team meets every Monday and Thursday at 9 AM for one hour. It is mandatory, starts and ends on time, and is run by my operations manager. Everyone gets their turn to bring up any ideas, suggestions, or challenges.

DD: What do you do to generate leads and which contact management system do you use?

DL: We generate leads by prospecting, lead follow-up, Zillow, Trulia, realtor.com, Holmes.com, for sale by owners, expired listings, and others. We use Top Producer as our contact management system.

DD: What do you think makes your team so successful?

DL: Hard work, passion, dedicated team members, following schedules, a fun working atmosphere. I am very serious about my business and it is run like a business, not a hobby.

DD: What are some of the distinctive marketing or advertising programs you use?

DL: My two sons, Jason and Drew, and I have come up with many different advertising and marketing pieces and programs. We have tested them, tracked them, edited them, and failed with many of them. We test and track everything we do. Now we have a list of letters and marketing pieces, a monthly newsletter, farm newsletters and marketing pieces, expired and for sale by owner marketing pieces, etc.

DD: In a sentence or two, could you describe your team's culture?

DL: We work hard, have fun, and support each other to offer the best real estate experience to our clients. The biggest asset of my team is the team members. Our motto is, "If you always do what is right for the client, in the end you win."

DD: How much importance do you place on training and coaching for your team members?

DL: I believe training and coaching of my team is critically important. I have a set schedule to train my agents and staff on an ongoing basis.

DD: What do you think is the biggest reason agents want to join your team?

DL: Agents join our team for several reasons. They make more money, they get to do the parts of their job they enjoy, they get lots of support staff to help them, and we have fun. Our team supports each other so well, especially when a team member goes on vacation. I encourage all of my team members to go on two to four vacations per year.

DD: When and if you lose a team member, is it more likely they leave, and if so why? Or that they are let go, and if so why?

DL: I believe that you should hire slow and fire fast. Of the agents and staff that I have had over the last 15 years, most of them stay with me for a very long time. I pay my staff more than the average and I treat them as one of the most important assets of our team.

DD: Do you allow or encourage teams within your overall team?

DL: No, not yet. I'm considering it with my top buyer agent right now.

DD: How important is it to your team which brokerage or brand you belong to?

DL: With everything that our team does, the brokerage or brand that we belong to is not very important at all. That being said, Engel and Völkers has been a very good fit for us, and that is why we joined them a few months ago. I believe our clients hire us, not our brokerage.

DD: How much volume does your team produce?

DL: Our goal is $60 million, with $75 million as our stretch goal and $100 million as our our Mamma Mia goal.

DD: How do you see real estate teams evolving in the future?

DL: With how complicated real estate is getting, along with the fact that technology is changing real estate and how we do business, I don't think individual agents are going to be able to compete with teams and therefore, teams will take over the real estate industry.

DD: How has the evolution of real estate teams changed our industry?

DL: Technology has changed the way real estate is being marketed and sold and it will never go back to the old way of selling real estate.

DD: Do real estate teams increase consumer service? And if so how?

DL: Yes, in today's very complicated real estate sales and marketing environment, having a team will absolutely give a better experience to our buyers and sellers and to all of our team members as well.

DD: Do you have plans on selling your team someday, and if so how will you go about that? Also, what do you believe teams in general need to do to increase their value?

DL: No, I don't see myself selling my business any time soon as I love real estate and am so passionate about it. That being said, I would like to build up my team so that it could be sold someday. In order to have a sellable business you must have a phenomenal database with very detailed information in it along with fantastic people. You must have all of your systems in place along with a policies and procedures manual for everything you do. If your entire business revolves around you, then you don't have anything to sell.

DD: How big can you see your team growing?

DL: I have hired three new agents in the last six months and we are at ten people right now. I don't see my team growing much more than where we are right now.

DD: Thank you David, for contributing from your wealth of knowledge on this topic. You have provided a fascinating, additional perspective.

A Nameless Team That 'Werks'

An interview with Felicia Werk Pavlica

Allan Dalton: What is your brand name?

Felicia Werk: It is just Felicia Werk Pavlica.

AD: How long have you been in business?

FW: About 15 years.

AD: What did you do before entering real estate?

FW: I came in shortly out of high school.

AD: How long were you in business before you added staff?

FW: I added full-time staff four years ago.

AD: What caused you to make that step?

FW: I felt that customer service was always important to me, my business, and my reputation, and I never wanted that to lapse. Therefore, I felt that if I could find somebody as dedicated as myself to serving my clients, that this would be good for me, my clients, and for that person. I also wanted to be certain to maintain as much balance in my personal life, to be able to give my clients the very best service, but not miss out on important moments with my family.

AD: What percentage of your personal attention is devoted to serving home sellers versus buyers?

FW: I would say 65% home sellers and 35% buyers.

AD: Who do you have assisting you now?

FW: I have a full time assistant, who is also my transaction coordinator, and a buyer's assistant, who is licensed. But she counts her transactions under her own name, making us unique in that we work our business together and yet separate.

AD: The reason why Debbie De Grote wanted to have you explain how you run your business is because you represent the thousands, if not tens of thousands, of agents who have assistants, specialists, and even buyer agents working with them full time, but who elect not to brand themselves as a team, as a group, or Felicia Werk Pavlica and Associates.

FW: A traditional team or large group is not the vision I have for my business at this time. I am very pleased with my small group and the very hands on approach I have with each client we service. I have watched countless people operate like me and call themselves a team, but it is not for me – it's not the vision I have for what I do.

AD: Well then, how does your vision for your small operation differ from all those who would define themselves as a team?
FW: I want consumers and clients to know that they will get me serving them, completely and always. If someone hires me, they do not have to worry about not being able to reach me or not having me there every step of the way. The specialization I am looking for is to how to best serve my clients. Client service is the team I am heading. This may change as time goes on, but due to where I am at in my personal life, this is how I feel now.

AD: And do you believe that shifting the focus on building a branded and larger team would distract from the high level of service which has been your standard and differentiator all these years?

FW: Absolutely, it would definitely force me to shift from that sacred obligation to my clients. I never take anything on partially, and if I hired more and grew my team, I would want them to be the best. I would be committed to helping and training them to get there. At this time, I am not able to offer that intensive training while also providing the level of service to my clients that I require, and furthermore while balancing family. What I have now is a better fit for me and my clients.

AD: How is your small, three-member, non-branded team presently doing?

FW: We closed the last year out with 165 transactions and $32,382,950 in sales volume.

AD: You are quite successful, and congratulations.

FW: In addition to my volume, my buyer agent closed 76 transactions and $12,448,480 in volume.

AD: How do you differentiate Felicia Werk Pavlica from the competition?

FW: I sell me, how I love what I do, my excitement for the success of each of my clients, my track record for success, and basically that I will be their real estate partner. I am honest and upfront with each person I am working for. I want to do whatever it takes to help them, and truly put myself in their shoes to best understand and help. I have a passion and want to see them succeed!

AD: It looks like you are a two person team with all of your clients.

FW: I want clients for life, referrals for life, and it all begins by the treating clients as partners.

AD: You seem to have more of a humanistic, so-called high touch approach versus high tech approach.

FW: You nailed it. Even though we take full advantage of all emerging technologies, first and foremost is understanding that we are representing human beings, with personal, lifestyle, and financial needs and concerns. It is imperative to connect first on that level. All of the technology is there just to facilitate how you can help them get there. And when you take care of the people, the money will follow, because money follows value.

AD: Sounds like your number one business system is the Golden Rule.

FW: You got it.

AD: What does you administrative person do?

FW: What doesn't Sue Bain do? This would be a better question, as she does everything. I do the selling, she makes sure every detail is addressed so that nothing gets missed, including managing my database. She is amazing and I am so grateful for her! I always mention how instrumental she is in my success.

AD: So, let me again make sure I understand your branding strategy. You want to constantly assure your local marketplace that when they turn to you, they have you to help them every step of the way. That you are their partner from start to finish, and hopefully for many more to come, I'm sure you would say.

FW: Yes, I want them to see me as their real estate partner as well as a local resource for anything needed.

AD: What can they get from you that they cannot get elsewhere?

FW: I know this may sound overly simplistic but it's like this: Imagine having your very best friend in the world, who also happens to be very successful in real estate, representing you. I want them to know that I am going to take care of them the way they would look out for their best friend or mom. And again, this is why it is important that I do not use the word team or group. It is crucial for me to have a hands-on approach with everyone so that I can make sure they are being cared for this way.

AD: I assume then that when you are coached, most of the coaching revolves around your personal business.

FW: Debbie helps me on all facets of our three person enterprise. Because we are in a small market, I learn from her constantly – like what top producers and teams are doing throughout the industry. She also keeps me focused, we all need that.

AD: Tell me about your market.

FW: I serve Kenosha, Wisconsin and our metropolitan population is about 150,000.

AD: How much of your business is done in Kenosha?

FW: I participated in 155 properties in Kenosha County and the remaining in Racine County.

AD: Since in Kenosha you have an area with 150,000 people, does that make it easier to reach and influence that territory than if there were 15 separate branded towns each with 10,000 folks? If your geography played out that way would you need to hire others to reach these differently branded and more distinct markets?

FW: That's a great question Allan. Yes, I believe we would.

AD: What are some of things you do for your community?

FW: Of all the things I do for the community, the number one priority is providing high level, quality real estate representation. I take pride in being helpful and a resource for anything needed.

AD: You mentioned you have children. How many and what are their ages?
FW: We have three children aged 16 years, 16 months, and our final on the way in October 2016.

AD: So your family has grown to be larger than your real estate team. Is your team at an ideal size for your market and for your vision of highly personal service?

FW: I always keep an open mind, but for now I love how I always have a complete hand and involvement in absolutely everything going on. When a buyer is working with Robbyn, even though she is a consummate professional, I am still involved with the progress.

AD: I believe strong agents and strong teams do best when they are part of strong companies. Tell me about the real estate company you are with.

FW: The RE/MAX company I work for has great ownership and leadership, great associates working for it, and we are number one in our area. RE/MAX is the best. They are a great brand and they really care about their agents. Everybody talks about finding your "why" these days, and I think the RE/MAX "why" was to free up Realtors from the restraints of yesteryear and empower them to reach their true potential.

AD: And what is your "why?"

FW: Debbie asks me this all the time and keeps bringing me back to it. My "why" is and always will be my family. From my father and mother, and by the way my mother made us a real estate family long before I did, to my own family of five. Everything I do is for them and to honor them.

Our Best Hope to Disrupt the Listing Side Disrupters: Real Estate Teams

By Allan Dalton

Membership in Mensa is not required to predict the following:

Real estate portals like Zillow, Realtor.com, and Trulia want to become the first and most trusted source not only for buyers, but for homeowners and home sellers as well.

Who can blame them?

The reason they have set their sights and sites on attracting home sellers is quite clear.

Specifically, they have concluded that if realtors will pay what they do for buyer leads, then they will pay considerably more for the more coveted listing side seller leads.

Disruption, according to Webster's Dictionary, means replacing the way things are done.

These aforementioned sites, thanks to the internet, have changed and disrupted the way in which buyers historically sought real estate information as they kicked off their home search.

Disruption on the buying side has not been as destructive to the real estate industry as the potential of listing side disruption. Where buying side disruption has had its most negative impact has been on the newspaper industry.

The days of buyers tolerating and squinting to see cryptic and abbreviated real estate ads, to the delight of both consumers and the real estate industry, are of the past. Instead, instant and robust images along with extensive text are now instantly available for all homes in all markets on both one's laptop and mobile.

That said, technology has also had an impact on the real estate industry by changing, or disrupting, the first point of contact with real estate buyers from the real estate industry to third party websites.

The impact of this disruption will be quite different on the selling side versus the buying side. This is because buying side disruption in real estate created both winners and losers. This disruption benefited both brokers.

The good news is that unlike the newspaper industry, the impact of buyer side disruption has been akin to a pebble in our collective shoes. Annoying yes, fatal no!

Especially when compared to the potentially devastating impact of listing side disruption. Those most devastated by listing side disruption would be the rain making listing agents and real estate teams.

Let's examine and compare disruption on the buying side versus the listing side.

This way we can determine if Debbie De Grote is on the money when she proclaims, as she has been for the past few years, that, "We need to disrupt the listing side disrupters."

First, here is why our industry was not disintermediated, never mind destroyed, by buying side disruption: It is because buying side disruption in real estate created winners and losers, or at best created a zero sum gain.

The winning brokers are:

1. Those real estate brokers who were able to make drastic cuts to their onerous classified newspaper advertising budgets.
2. Those real estate brokers (not all) who were able to recover from higher commission splits through having their agents pay for their own internet advertising.
3. Those brokers who were able to monetize internet traffic through in house company referral programs, when they were not able to charge for referrals through the classified newspaper and floor time format.

Now let's take a look at why we need to disrupt the listing side disrupters. Top producing teams rely upon the following:

1. Their listings generating leads through their database, versus the past when company driven newspaper advertising generated

leads for the whole company.
2. Their listings creating many more buyers, enabling teams to hire buyer agents.
3. Being the first point of contact with home sellers (instead of Zillow, Realtor.com, Trulia, etc.) Real estate teams were formed because of the need of buyer agents to service leads.

Therefore, it should come as no surprise that the development of real estate teams essentially came at the same time as the development of the web. Essentially everything else stayed the same.

Beyond the financial concerns of our industry, clearly the consumer was thrilled. Home sellers obtained more exposure for their properties and buyers enjoyed a better consumer experience,

For their part, brokers reduced their ad costs and their agents, who were now paying for their own internet ads, were able to do so through historically high commission splits

While I was at Realtor.com, I introduced company showcase to the industry for those brokers who wanted to advertise their listings and to gain more traffic for everyone in the company. And they could also control or monetize the leads.

The winning top producers and teams are those who:

1. Their listings generate leads to their contact information versus being subsumed by the company at-large floor time distribution.
2. Their listings created many more buyers, leading to the hiring of buyer agents by top listing agents.
3. Hiring buyer agents led to real estate team formation.

The buying side disruption ironically favored and helped listing agents to further dominate.

Now let us turn to the adverse impact of widespread listing side disruption.

1. Marketing Fees

Essentially, all real estate fees are negotiable (which will be the issue) and are decided upon by the listing/marketing agent and home seller.

This means that there is very little, if any, involvement with the buyer when it comes to influencing fees. Therefore, losing first point of contact with sellers who may be influenced on fees by the disrupters will have a major impact.

Therefore, the prospects of home selling consumers being profoundly influenced as they begin to prepare to sell by third party sites regarding a menu of real estate fees is foreboding.

Picture ads such as, "Find out who sells the most in your area and who charges the least," will unquestionably change the way marketing fee decisions are traversed.

Now if that ad describes how you want to be portrayed then that would be welcomed disruption, but I doubt that is a message that most successful real estate teams want to see as commonplace.

2. Real Estate Domination

This virtually always begins and is sustained on the listing side. This will be in peril if listing side disruption is not counter veiled by powerful real estate teams.

Think about it, how many top producers, especially before the advent of buyer agent assistants, did you ever hear proclaim, "I do not want to work with any more sellers, just buyers." Instead, it was "I don't want to work with buyers."

The reason why real estate teams and groups are best suited to contact home sellers before the real estate portals do is because top team leaders and top producing listing agents are virtually always:

> A. More strategic
> B. More marketing oriented
> C. More prospecting oriented
> D. More networking oriented
> E. More referral oriented
> F. More personal promotion oriented
> G. More contact management oriented
> H. And are the modern day hunter gatherers versus either buyer agents or most of the real estate agents desperately looking for leads from the internet.

Essentially all of these aforementioned skills, along with the team leader's selling skills, are monumentally more useful, efficient, and effective in targeting home sellers than when employed in the courting of buyers. This is because potential sellers are more identifiably located and, therefore, prospecting oriented agents can direct efforts towards engaging them.

Accordingly, prospective home sellers can be systematically and relentlessly engaged before they turn to the internet and decide to sell. Buyers, on the other hand, typically make their presence and location known, be it anywhere in the world, only in conjunction with when they begin to search for property.

The ease of identifying potential home sellers versus the elusive nature of determining where buyers might be coming from is why listings are far more effectively and disproportionately controllable than buyers by most real estate teams.

Moreover, buyers are typically disproportionately attracted by the degree that one disproportionately captures listings.

Therefore, if third party sites insert themselves first and foremost with sellers, the outcome may not be a welcomed one for most real estate team leaders who excel at capturing listings.

Picture a world (it has already begun) which thrusts prospective home sellers into an environment of imperfect and, at times, laughable and compromised real estate ratings and reviews.

Of course, the disruption doesn't stop there. It extends into how many homes were sold on their street and by whom, homes sold in their price range along with the fees being charged, and then the ads move on to explore the relative range of fees being charged. Additionally, they will be focused on which real estate certifications and designations are most meaningful to home sellers.

When a real estate top producer believes they would, hands down, win all of the aforementioned advertised selection criteria, then of course listing side disruption would benefit them.

You would gladly give up the first point of contact to a third party so called "objective" site where they shine above all others and in all categories, including lowest fees charged. For most listing agents, however, this type of advertised selection criteria would, without question, be disruptive.

Therefore, such strategic insertion with potential home sellers will disrupt the present landscape and ecosystem in which top listing agents and team leaders have flourished. However, unlike where buyers gain from buying side disruption, the consumer advantage here will be dubious.

My assertion is based on the fact that typically a top producing agent or team leader is such because they have demonstrated a proven capacity to make things happen, resolve problems, and arrive at solutions and deliver favorable outcomes for their clients.

For example, someone might sell 100% of their listings because they only had four for the year and all sold. Does this mean they are the best? Well, in one criterion, unfortunately, yes. This is why a heavy price will be paid if homeowners believe that the internet will present them with the best agents, as it does now in presenting all properties.

These talents of top producers are what caused them to become a top listing agent and/or a top real estate team leader. The consumer will not always arrive at this conclusion as these websites seek to inform consumers that they know best, and who the best choices are.

Here is why Debbie De Grote and I believe that real estate teams, and specifically team leaders, represent the best hope to stop, slow down, or disrupt these listing side disrupters.

First of all, the best chance at keeping listing side first point of contact is through personal and trusted engagement at the local level. Real estate teams do this best.

Real estate team leaders, for the most part, have become successful through mastering this localized prospecting and marketing process.

Because real estate teams are typically more intensely localized than their brokerage (especially large regional brokerages) they are our best hope to deploy team resources to create sustainable community based connections.

Second, real estate teams, because their genesis is typically that of a top listing agent, have developed contact management systems that can be extended throughout the team. Companies typically leave contact management systems up to their agents, but most non-listing agents do not do enough business so they do not reach critical contact management mass.

Most agents are distracted and are disproportionately focused on social media. They gravitate to social media more than to localized prospecting, networking, and marketing, all geared to prospective listings. This is because brands, brokers, and industry-wide technological advances are geared more towards attracting buyers.

Top producers and team leaders cannot sustain their success in most instances through a 50/50 relationship with buyers and sellers. For those who can, most would agree that their 50% of buyers are more a result of their listings than the reverse.

Third, real estate team leaders are more likely to be able to perform as modern day feudal lords and barons dispensing fiefs or "farms" to team members than are brokers or office managers. This is because brokers and office managers cannot afford to attempt to split up territories among hundreds in the same local market, but teams can manage this localized farm and approach much better.

Because geographical territories cannot be dispensed within larger offices, this oftentimes creates an office-wide farming or prospecting like atrophy. The result of this is no one ends up truly cultivating a geographical area replete with numerous potential home seller listings. This makes it more likely that home owners can and will be tagged up stream, so to speak, by websites addressing their home selling and homeownership related content and advertising.

Therefore, companies cannot create laser like localized marketing, networking, social media, prospecting, and overall farming effort, which is required to prevent disruption from online sites, but real estate teams can and must.

The fourth point is that real estate companies are more likely to hire a director of social media than a director of prospecting.

Real estate teams place an immensely higher level of importance on door knocking, telemarketing, mailings, community participation, and overall prospecting than a company generally does. Teams do this while also engaging heavily into social media marketing.

All of these reasons and many more represent why real estate teams are uniquely equipped to maintain and grow their listing side dominance. This will be the way to disrupt the listing side disrupters in their local market.

Real estate teams, in my view will need to make two major changes to preemptively inoculate themselves from the influence of third party websites who seek to control the first point of contact with potential home sellers in their communities.

1. Become much more strategic in their approach. (Ask us for a copy of how to develop a community marketing business plan)
2. Create compelling, consumer-centric off and online content and consumer guides that relate to all marketplace needs. That is, to professionally address that which homeowners and local buyers want to know before, during, and after the transaction.

For the past year I have been working with Debbie and marketing and technology guru Pete Mitchell on the development of the Real Estate Teams' Community Customized Marketing System.

This system includes consumer guides, webinars, and online content including topics such as:

- Downsizing with Distinction
- How to Know When It's Time to Move Up
- Your Real Estate Planning Guide
- Is It Better to Rent or Own a Home?
- There is Only One Reason Why a Home Has Not Sold . . . (Yet) Ineffective Marketing
- A Home Seller's Guide to Selecting the Right Real Estate Agent to Market Your Home
- How to Convert From Just Selling Your Home to Having It Professionally Marketed
- Neighbors Know Best (a neighborhood review program)
- Maximizing Home Sale Value When Divorcing
- Selecting the Right Real Estate Professional to Buy or Sell Your Investment Property

As well as how to create local marketing events, create a community website or video, and much, much more.

While there have been others (too few) who have produced consumer off and online guides with similar purposes and titles, as you will see, nothing to date in our industry approaches the consumer in the compelling manner that our content makes possible.

We believe real estate teams are not only the best hope to maintain the listing side control we desperately need, but also that real estate teams are the most natural home for our system and content.

In summary, there is no doubt in my mind, for all of the aforementioned reasons, that real estate teams are not only the best hope to disrupt listing side disruption, but quite possibly, maybe the only hope.

Meet Mr. Social Media

An interview with Pete Mitchell

Debbie De Grote: Pete, I'd like to talk to you about what is one of the most asked about topics of real estate team leaders. What is the best way to leverage social media?

Pete Mitchell: Well, first of all, I want to be clear. It is not possible in just one interview to cover all you need to know about social media. We should though, try to cover at least some of the best practices.

DD: Where should a real estate team leader begin on the subject of social media?

PM: The first thing I want to cover in your social media best practices is choosing the social media platform that is right for you. You've got to ask yourself, what social media platform do I like? So if you're already engaged in Facebook or Pinterest or YouTube or Twitter, then obviously that's a social media platform that I would encourage you to continue to use. What I wouldn't do is go after a social media platform because you think you should be there and you're just not.

Social media might be the hot topic of the day. Even though social media represents a transcendent movement, that does not for a minute mean that's where most business comes from for real estate agents. It does not even mean that's where the majority of business comes from, because a majority of real estate business does not come from social media. It comes from traditional advertising. It comes from direct mail, which actually is the number one source. It comes from doing all of the things that you've always been doing, like door knocking, cold calling, things like that. People don't like to hear that. They want to hear that there is a magic bullet, that if they pull out the magic gun they can shoot the magic bullet and it just gets them business. If life were that easy, then real estate would not pay as well as it does. It would pay minimum wage and everyone would do it. So again, I encourage you to look at the social media platforms that you currently like to use.

The other qualifier that I look for is looking for your demographic, meaning who do you normally work with or who do you like working with? Your ideal target audience is what we would call this. Are they on a social media platform and if they are, which ones are they on? So for instance, all age groups are on Facebook, but Millennials are one of the lighter groups on Facebook. So if you work with seniors, maybe you work with seniors who downsize or move to senior communities, if that is your target market you are going to find them on Facebook. If fact, you're probably going to find them on Facebook more than you are on any other social media network. That's because for them to stay connected with their kids and their grandkids they had to get on Facebook and that's why they chose to do.

If you work in commercial real estate then I would strongly suggest Facebook because business owners are on Facebook and, of course, LinkedIn, which is the forgotten social media network because it's primarily for business people. If you work with women primarily, maybe they are single moms, or just single females, then I would look towards Pinterest because that has a majority of women on there as opposed to men. If you worked with say, celebrities or in the Hollywood area, then I might look to Twitter to make my presence known because a lot of celebrities are on Twitter.

If your market is Millennials, then I would definitely look to Instagram. I would look to Snapchat, and yes, Snapchat actually does have an advertising feature which is one that, the more I look at, the more I really like. The reason for that is, the way Snapchat works, if you haven't used Snapchat, is if someone sends you a Snap, you only have it on your phone for a few seconds before it's deleted forever. So when you run ads on Snapchat, what's happening is you're getting people's undivided attention for those few precious seconds when they're actually looking at what you've sent. I really like that idea because to have someone's undivided attention, to get them to say, yes I want this, no I don't want this, or I'm going to click and find out about this website or something like that, that could be a really big push. So you might go, well Millennials right now, they don't have the means to buy homes. It depends. Again, it depends on where you are at. So if you were in the Silicon Valley, for instance, I would go after Millennials because a lot of Millennials do work in the tech industry and in the industries that surround the tech industries, and they do a lot of times have money. So if that were my market and that's where I lived, I would be looking to Instagram. I would be looking to Snapchat.

DD: What are your thoughts regarding real estate and YouTube?

PM: We sometimes under leverage YouTube because we primarily think about it as a video site, but it's really interesting to see how the playing field has changed over the years with YouTube. Kind of what I mean by that is Millennials today won't sign up for cable. It boggles my mind, but they will literally sit and watch whole shows and movies on their cell phone. Now, you've got to understand, you're talking to a guy who literally has a 100-inch screen that I watch all of my TV and movies on. So the idea of watching something on a 4-inch screen is kind of like, why in the world would I do that? But that's not my generation. The Millennials are the ones that really like that kind of thing.

So if you were constantly putting out content on YouTube that might be a great way again, not just to reach Millennials, but everyone who uses YouTube. In fact, it's the #2 search engine. So people go on YouTube and they will type in "how to buy a home" or something like that, and if you had content out there that you were able to get ranked in YouTube, your videos can come up. That does not mean it's going to be targeted content because hey, if someone's trying to buy a home in New Jersey and you live in Phoenix, Arizona, what do you care if your video came up and helped them? They're not going to be the right person for you. It's one of those social media platforms that I wouldn't ignore. In my financial planning business which is how I got started in all the marketing, I put out videos on how the stock market worked, how annuities worked, things like that. Some of those got ranked. Some didn't. It was kind of like a crap shoot and I still get calls from people who watch those videos even today. Unfortunately, the calls are from literally all over the country and in financial planning I could only take you on as a client if you were in California.

So anyway, the #1 social media best practice is that you've got to choose the social media platform you want to use. Those are just some criteria. I would encourage that if you like Facebook at all, stay with Facebook and use that one because it has the largest amount of people on it from all demographics, so it's really a good place to be for social media.

DD: Pete, a lot of real estate team leaders ask me about whether they should focus more on organic or paid marketing online, what do you say?

PM: That's a good question. Let's start with what you mean by organic, and use Facebook as an example. You go on there and every once in a while you post something. This just happened with your kids, maybe you put up a picture or a video or a quote, or you share someone else's. That's all organic Facebook marketing. It's just being organic on Facebook. On the other hand, paid marketing is that you are literally paying to have your message, your advertisement, run on Facebook. Decide which one of those you're going to primarily focus on and then go for it.

Organic marketing, which is free, usually takes a significantly longer period of time in which to generate a lead and then to generate a client. In real estate you might be looking at 9 months to even a year if all you're doing is organic marketing on Facebook, whereas with paid marketing on Facebook I can literally start running my ad in a few minutes and start generating leads a few minutes after that. Then, of course, if I'm generating leads now, how much longer does that mean I need to wait before I'm able to convert some of those leads into clients? It's usually considerably shorter, anywhere from days to weeks, sometimes maybe 2 months to convert someone to being a client as opposed to organic which might take me 9+ months in order to make that happen.

Of course, if you don't have much money then you do the organic. But if you've got more money than you do time, then I would say do paid placement. Personally, I love paid placement because Facebook really lets you zero in and show your ads to your ideal client. Again, this isn't the training for everything to know about Facebook advertising. If you would like to know more about that, go to the Excelleum.com website. Click over to the Events page and see if we have a Facebook training coming up. It is not a free training when we do it over there. It is a paid training. However, there is just so much material that we cover on that training that if that is something that interests you, that's where I would direct you to go.

DD: Pete, I love your long and comprehensive answers, because social media is a very complex subject and to properly understand it means understanding its many nuances. So let me ask you now about something you and I were talking about the other day, live streaming. Is this something real estate teams should look into?

PM: Absolutely. There are several platforms now that allow you to broadcast video live as you're doing it. The three main ones today, and this could change because social media is one of those things that grows and dies all the time, but the three main ones today are Facebook Live, Periscope, and YouTube streaming. Each of these has their pros and cons. Facebook Live is really so new at this point that who knows what it's going to change to in the future. The reason why I like it is again there are so many people on Facebook that streaming live on Facebook is really, really cool. Whereas Periscope, which is kind of like a subsidiary of Twitter, again Twitter is one of those things . . . it's dying. I don't care what anyone says. It is dying. Periscope to me is really, really cool. I really like it. I don't know if that's enough to save Twitter or not. It might be and if it is, that's awesome. YouTube streaming, again, you could do live broadcasts on YouTube if you wanted.

If this is something that you chose to do, what you want to do for your live streaming is you want to decide, okay, what kind of content do I want to put out and how often do I want to put it out? Then you want to be consistent. Let's say you live in Costa Mesa, California or your geographic farm is somewhere in Costa Mesa, California, and you wanted to put out a video every Monday on living in Costa Mesa. You could put out videos where you say, "Hey, these are the homes that came on the market this last week. We've got a 3 bedroom, 2 bath. I went and saw it. It's really gorgeous inside. I think the back yard needs a little bit of work. It looks like if you want to take on a house that's going to have a little bit of work in cleaning up the back yard, this would be the one for you. It reflects it in the price."

You could really just talk about the homes that just came on the market. That's going to attract a certain type of person to you. So, for instance, if you did a lot of open houses and you friended all of the people who showed up at the open houses in your Facebook account, and then started doing videos like this, that's another great way to connect with people. There is nothing to say that you couldn't do all 3. You could do Facebook and you could do YouTube and you could do Periscope. I don't know of a way to do the video once and have it live stream on all 3. Someone will eventually make a tool for that I am sure, and then I would say that's the way to go. You're just going to get it out there in multiple places all at once. But that is something that you can consider if you're going to do live streaming.

DD: I suspect that many of my top producing and real estate team leader clients might be too busy to do live streaming on a consistent basis by themselves. But one of the many benefits of building a bigger, busier, and more profitable real estate team is to be able to delegate important functions like these to other team members or dedicated staff. Now let me ask you to explain to our readers what you mean when you talk about the 90/10 rule. Is this where you're talking about 10% of the business is done by 90% of the realtors? Or something else?

PM: Debbie, my 90/10 rule in this case, refers to how 90% of the time I want to see real estate teams focusing on providing your friends, fans, and followers with great content.

DD: Why is this so important?

PM: Real estate professionals need to understand that social media is not just what I call "a pitch fest," where on every post you are trying to pitch them on the new home or on why they should list with you. Remember, people are on social media first and foremost to connect with you, and not be sold by you. So if you were to do live streaming, give them great content and only at the very end go and by the way, if you'd like help finding any of these homes or if you would like to list your own home feel free to call me. Here's my phone number. Here's my website. That's about the most that I want you to do on live streaming and when it comes to generic posts on Facebook, I would say 9 content posts for every 1 sale or offer related post.

Now again, this doesn't apply to advertising. This is just for the organic side - 90/10. Nine great posts, great content, once every 10 times, you're going to then run an offer or tell them about using you or something like that.

DD: Since you called this a 90/10 rule, let's keep with that theme. What is another vital rule for real estate team leaders to observe?

PM: To give great value before asking for anything. This is very much like what I just talked about. You want to go for the 9 great posts before you hit them up with your offer. You've got to be focused on value. You have to care more about your followers, your fans, your clients, your prospects than you do about you. People will sense that. When you're constantly delivering great value to them, they really want to pay attention.

A great example of this is you and Excelleum. We do several webinars every month for our list, and it's always great content that we're focusing on and then at the very end we'll offer usually a strategy call with one of your coaches or something like that. We're focused on giving great content first. That's what we want to go for.

DD: Well, we couldn't do it without you. What else do you have for us, Pete?

PM: Next is the importance of the real estate team leader or member's profile picture. Now, all the social media platforms are going to allow you to have a profile picture. So on Facebook this, of course, is that little picture that everyone sees. Usually you put a picture of you. Some people put a picture of their dog or their kids or something like that. Since you're in real estate I want you to have a picture with you. I don't care if it's a picture with you and your significant other. I don't care if it's a picture of you and Fido. I don't even care if it's really a picture of you having fun. This is social media. But I want you to really pay attention to the image that you're projecting publicly. I think it's great if you have a fun image. I think it's great if people can see you and they can see you with your significant other because, again, this is social media. I think when we've got the professional headshot as a profile picture you look too stuffy. You look like you're all business all the time. I don't think that's good on social media. I don't care if you're wearing a suit, but let's not do the same headshot that you do on all your business cards and everything else. Let's have fun. This is social. We want people to see us as a real person, not just as a sales professional.

Also, I want you to be consistent on all of your social media platforms. So if you said, hey, I'm going to use LinkedIn, I'm going to use Twitter, and I'm going to use Facebook, same profile picture on all of them. The reason for that is this is where your branding starts to come into place. I want people to remember you and this is where branding does matter, right? Because they are getting to know you. So a lot of times when I start saying this to people they go, wait a second Pete, I thought you were all about direct response marketing and you hated branding? No. I don't hate branding. I just think everyone does it at the wrong time. This is the time that you want to be wary of your brand and the image that you're projecting.

Be very careful what you post and what you say in your post. What I mean by that is I don't care if you are a liberal or you are a conservative and you want to post about that stuff. Great marketing repels as much as it attracts. So let's just say you were really, really liberal and everything you posted was all about liberal agenda items, you are going to repel all of the conservative people and you are going to attract all the liberal people. That's a good thing because you're probably going to connect best with them. I'm not afraid of offending people online. I mean I don't think you should be rude, but I'm not worried about if they're like, oh you know what, I can't stand this person because the reality is that I want us to have a relationship. So I'm totally okay with that. If you're really conservative and you're like, I think everyone by law should have to carry a gun with them and the government should be out and taxation is theft and all the conservative issues and positions, that's fine too because again, you're going to repel everyone who's liberal but you're going to attract to yourself everyone who's conservative.

When I say you need to be careful what you post online, what I am more concerned with is how you come across when you state these things. I would say that you want to stay away and I almost can't believe I have to say this, but I do because I've got a lot of real estate agents who are friends of mine on Facebook. Please don't be profane in your posts. I know that's almost like absurd that I have to say that. This is your public face. If you go, well I don't actually friend any of my clients or prospects. Well, you might think that you're not friending them, but they are searching for you. If your privacy settings aren't right and people are actually seeing some of the posts that you put up, maybe it's you drunk at the bar, you know, do I really want to use someone for my most important investment, the biggest amount of money I'm ever going to spend, and I know last night they were out drunk at a bar and they're cussing left and right on their Facebook post? I'm not going to use that person. It's so unflattering.

DD: Pete, I love the advice. Let's keep moving on. What's next?

PM: The importance of posting frequency. I'm going to tell you, this is going to vary by platform. For instance, if you're doing Twitter you need to be posting a lot, I mean, at least 7 to 10 times a day. One of the reasons for that is your tweet is going to get lost so quick, I mean so quick. It's not going to sit around and people aren't going to see it, so you need to be doing 7 to 10 tweets a day if you're on Twitter. If you're on Facebook, I'm going to tell you that you want to do a minimum of 1 a day. I would say that you want to vary the times that you put it out, and you're going to start finding out what gets the best response.

DD: So should team leaders be posting as their personal account, or on their business fan page on Facebook?

PM: The answer to that is you kind of need to do both. Facebook tells you right off the bat that your business page, all of the people who like that page, the fans and the followers of that page, out of that group only about 15% are ever going to see your posts. They deliberately throttle all of that because they want you to do paid advertising. Makes sense, that's their business model, so just be okay with that. Your friends, the people who are going to see it are the ones that you interact with the most. So you do want to be interacting with them, and you want them to be interacting with you. So if you see someone post something really cool on Facebook, go ahead and comment on it, like it, share it, things like that, and they will return the favor for you.

One of the things that I like to do is when I put out a post and someone comments on it, I always like their comment unless they're being a jerk in which case I might actually just ban them if they're being a jerk because who needs that in your life, right? But even if they disagree with me, I'll like the comment because I want to be social on Facebook. I want to be social in social media. I want people to listen to me and I want to listen to other people. So I always like their comments when they comment on anything that I post. If you're doing LinkedIn, things of that nature, you can get away with a little bit less. Again, I would still say once a day, but it is okay if you do a blog post and you're only doing maybe 2 to 3 of those a week, like a Monday, Wednesday, Friday type deal, you can get away with that. But again, just keep in mind that the more you post, the better chance you have at creating relationship and getting social interaction with people. That is one of the things that you really want to be doing when you're doing social media.

DD: Great. Now let me ask you to review how teams or leaders should actually manage their profile.

PM: Well, when you're filling out your profile online, and every social media site has some form of profile, I want you to be as complete as possible. So I want you to put on there your website. If you have landing pages for consumer guides or for home values, I want you to put those on there as well, you know, as many as the social media platform will let you do. I say go ahead and do it. It's not going to hurt you, and it can only help you. I would have your authority website, your main website, as the #1 link because again, this is social media. I want to attract potential sellers and potential buyers to me, and the best way for me to do that is to show them my authority at this point, in this stage of the game. So I'm going to have a link to my main website there, and that's what I'm going to be doing with that.

The rest of your profile should be as complete as possible. That does not mean you have to share everything. So what I mean by that is if you're like, hey, I don't want to give away my birth date. I feel kind of awkward with that, then don't. That's cool. I would at least fill it out and then tell Facebook or Twitter, don't show this part of my profile. Turn that part off. I believe on my profile I have the date but I don't have the year, which is kind of stupid because I mean in today's day and age of identity theft they're going to get both. They're going to figure out, oh, okay well you graduated in this year. That means you must be this old and so that means your year of birth is this. So I'm kind of torn. I actually have one friend who has a completely fake birth date on social media because they just don't want people to know. I get that from an identity theft standpoint. That is one of those things that I am okay with.
DD: Let's now move specifically to the Facebook business page.

PM: What I would suggest for you is to have a minimum of 2 pages. I've got a whole bunch of pages, and I use them differently. But one of the Facebook pages I would encourage you to have would be a community page. So I might call it, like I live in a little city called Rossmoor, so I might call it Rossmoor community. Now, I don't have that because I don't sell real estate in Rossmoor and I have no desire to do that for this area, but if I did in this area I would have that page.

In this Rossmoor community page, I would literally put as much info as I could about what's going on in Rossmoor. So for instance, every summer they have movies in the park. One of our parks here, they have the big screen that comes and they blow it up and all the families bring their kids and their lawn chairs. Everyone sits out there and they watch movies. It's usually like a kids' movie, a cartoon. I would put all of that information on this community site, and I would boost the page to people who live in Rossmoor who had that zip code. I would try and get them to like it. I would use a tagline for the page along the lines of, "always know what's going on Rossmoor" or "keeping you connected with what's going on in Rossmoor," so that way when people see this page, they're like, oh, okay, well I live in Rossmoor, I want to know what's going on in Rossmoor, I'm going to go ahead and like this page.

Then I would constantly be putting content up on that page. In real estate, I might start including homes that are for sale on that page even if they're not my listings. I would talk about, "hey this home just hit the MLS." Now you've got to follow your rules, what's okay for you to do with your MLS, if you need to contact the other agent. I'm going to leave that up to you. You know what the rules are in your state, your area, your community, what your broker wants you to do, and if you don't, you need to ask your broker. But I would put up stuff like that. I would put up every time there is a school event, every time there is a church event, every time there is a carnival that comes to your community, every time the Lions group does something, or the Kiwanis group, or whatever it might be, that's where I'm going to be posting all of that stuff. That gets you connected.

The second type of Facebook business page that I would have would be so I can run ads on Facebook. I could always run it under the Rossmoor community page, but I kind of want to leave that untouched and untainted. I don't want people to think, oh, okay, this guy is just setting up this page so they can run ads or market to me, so I don't want to like it. So I would set up a business page, and I wouldn't call it Pete Mitchell Real Estate. I would actually just call it "Pete Mitchell" and I would use the same profile picture that I use for my regular Facebook page.

People ask me all the time. They go, why do you do that? The main reason that I do it is I like to run ads that show up in someone's newsfeed. So the newsfeed is that main thing right in the middle of Facebook, right, and if you look closely enough at some posts they will say up in the corner "sponsored." That means it's an ad. When it comes from Pete Mitchell Realty people automatically know it's an ad, but when it comes from Pete Mitchell sometimes they think, oh this might be someone that I friended. What are they saying? So they are not immediately turned off by it, and that's why I really like the idea of having a Facebook business page that I can run ads under that is the same as my name. I want people to basically think oh, well this is a post from Pete Mitchell. I don't want them to think, oh, well this is clearly an advertisement. So that's why I do that.

Now, for the content that I put on that page, it's going to be the same content that I put on my Rossmoor community page. I'm always going to have content on there. I'm always going to be putting content on there. I don't want to be using a blank page because what some people will do is they click actually on that link to go who is Pete Mitchell, I don't remember him, and it's going to take him back to your business page and I want them to actually see there is content on there, not that I am basically starting it to run ads, which is what I'm trying to do, but I don't want them to have that as their first impression.

DD: Pete, you have covered organic content. I can't end this interview without asking you to provide our readers with some of your considerable wisdom regarding the subject of paid advertisements.

PM: Here's the deal. Organic takes a long time to get a client. We have already talked about that. It can take you 9+ months to get a client when all you're doing is organic marketing. I would say to you, consider running ads because you can get a lead today that you might be able to convert tomorrow so you can get paid 30 days from now, right. So I like paid advertisements. When you have more time than money, do all the organic stuff. When you have more money than time, do all the paid stuff. That's just going to basically help you make more money quicker. So I love running ads. I run ads all the time. There's a lot of different ways that you can run ads. There are lots of different objectives you can have when you're running ads. You can run ads for open houses, which we do a lot. You can run ads for your consumer guides. You can run ads to generate leads. You can run ads for home values. Lots of different styles of ads that you can run.

But I would say consider doing paid ads. It can be some of the best money that you spend and some of the quickest turnaround. You can also decide how much you want to spend, meaning $5 a day I believe is the minimum that you can do with no daily limit. I mean there is no minimum days, I should say, so if you just wanted to just spend $5 you could spend $5. Usually when we do open house ads we'll spend $50, and we'll generate a ton of people through the home and the main reason is ironically not to sell the home, it is actually to get us another listing. But that is something that we'll cover in more detail on the Facebook training that we'll do at another time.

DD: Well Pete, I not only want to thank you, I want to also say how proud I am that you are an important part of the Excelleum Coaching & Consulting faculty. How about giving us a checklist regarding a social media strategy?

PM:
1. Choose a social media platform you want to be use.
2. Decide if you're going to do organic or paid marketing.
3. Do live streaming whenever possible.
4. Stick to the 90/10 rule of 90% content and 10% being sales or your offer.
5. Give great value before asking for anything.
6. Keep your profile picture consistent across all social media platforms and keep it social, not just business related.
7. Posting frequency: You need to be doing multiple posts a day if you're on Twitter. Three times a week would be great on LinkedIn, and, of course, at least daily if you're on Facebook.
8. Keep your profile up to date and always make sure your website is the #1 thing that everyone can find on your social media profile.
9. Set up a Facebook business page using just your name, and maybe a community page too.
10. Consider running paid ads.

Teams and Coaching:
A Match Made in Heaven

By Debbie De Grote

Take a minute to think about your favorite team, in any sport. They, as all do, have a coach or multiple coaches, don't they? Even though they may already be outstanding performers, they know that they often cannot see their own flaws, and even if they are aware of those flaws, they may not be objective enough or have the knowledge needed to know how to correct the flaws and streamline their processes. They also know that sometimes the difference in winning and losing is nothing more than a fraction of a second. They have to be at their best. They have to be better than the rest, and a great coach can be the key ingredient in a stellar career.

Often I am asked why would team leaders whose teams are producing $100, $150, and even $400 million in sales volume hire Excelleum to coach them. What they are really asking is what would these super salespeople have left to learn? These super salespeople would probably respond with, "A lot!" Because they have big goals and even bigger dreams, and the bigger you want to be, the more guidance, fresh ideas, and input you need.

What I always point out to anyone asking this question is that top performers are never satisfied. They are always looking for the next mountain to climb, and no matter how good they are they need a guide to get them to the top.

The real estate industry is becoming more competitive every day. In fact, soon the 80/20 Rule (20% of the agents do 80% of the business) will be shifting to the 90/10 Rule (10% of the agents will be doing 90% of the business). In an article I read on this topic, it stated that 90% of the top 10% have at least one coach. I assume that because you are taking the time to read this book, you want to be in that top 10% that out performs all the rest. And why not, right? Someone has to do it, why can't it be you? If the statistic is accurate that 90% of the top 10% have a coach, I wonder who is coaching you.

In his book *The E-Myth*, Michael Gerber talks about the fact that most entrepreneurs have never been taught to build a systematic, turn key business. They are great rainmakers and highly skilled technicians, and yet they often struggle to build a business that works even when they don't. I love the story in the book about the famous pie maker that was told by everyone to open a pie shop. However, when she took that advice and did so, she failed. Why? Because making pies is not the same as running a pie shop. Selling a lot of houses is not the same as building and running a team.

At Excelleum we help the team leaders define their vision. This takes them beyond just how much money they want to make this year or next; this takes us to the finish line, where they want to end up, and then allows us to work backwards to construct the plan to get them there. Once the vision and the plan are in place, we next conduct a business overhaul to identify gaps in their current processes and help them maximize their results in their areas of strength. We explore areas of additional opportunity, review their existing staff, and help them vet potential hires.

Once the customized success blueprint is complete, we hold the entire team accountable to stay the course and help them make adjustments as needed along the way.

I certainly must also mention that the team leader and everyone on the team takes the DISC assessment so that each team member is carefully and accurately selected for their role and is placed in the best position possible to contribute to the team's success and achieve their own personal goals.

There is another reason that most top producers and top teams hire a coach. They realize that to survive and thrive they need to differentiate themselves in the market. They know they need help to determine how to do so, because they know they need to compete against other agents in their company, other brands, other top producers, and certainly against other teams. They need a competitive edge that quality coaching can provide.

In fact, coaching is, without question, the ultimate differentiator. Why? First of all, it plays into the strength of the team leader who, in most instances, evolved into their status due to their prolific rainmaking skill and needs help balancing all of the demands that managing and developing a team places on their shoulders.

Moreover, the office manager is not set up for the same level of intimacy with the team members and may not personally have the experience needed to provide advice and guidance to the team leader. In most cases they simply cannot provide the high level, specialized, and personalized coaching most teams desperately need.

I actually believe that without this type of high level coaching many of the high powered teams of today would not exist. I have noticed that even in just the last two to three years teams across the nation are stepping up their commitment to coaching, not just for the team leader but also for every member on their team.

Why Don't Their Brokers Coach Them?

Some managers and brokers do coach their agents, or at least attempt to. The reason I say attempt to is because even though some brokers and managers are more than willing to help, the team leader rejects their help, preferring instead to consult with a neutral expert.

Sometimes brokers may even be intimidated by the teams, perhaps because they themselves were not top producers or team owners. They feel they just do not have much to share that will be valuable to the team's growth. Even if the manager or broker was a top producer, chances are it has been years, and over time the way agents approach team building has changed dramatically.

The brokers, unfortunately, do not have the same opportunity that my coaches and I do to speak with hundreds of team leaders and team experts a year. They don't have the time to be immersed in the study of team trends and expansion plans and other new and cutting edge team strategies the way we do.

In fact, many wonderful and caring brokers reach out to us to connect us to their teams, asking us to step in and assist because they want to help, they just don't know where to begin when it comes to building mega teams.

I thought I would wrap up this discussion on teams and coaching by sharing an interview with a terrific real estate agent, who is actually a member of one of the family teams interviewed in this book. He also happens to be an Olympic athlete. I thought you would enjoy his thoughts on coaching, as he sums it up quite nicely.

Navigating the Downhill Slopes of Real Estate

An interview with Erik Schlopy

Debbie De Grote: Erik is part of a well-known real estate family and he is now stepping into the real estate world. To be an athlete, how many hours and pain and coaches and discipline that takes, and we can't even pick up the phone and prospect! Maybe you can give some thoughts about that.

Erik Schlopy: I broke my back in a crash at the world championships in Japan in 1993. I swung wide on a turn and was going about 70 mph when I hit a compression I didn't know was there. I went 280 feet in the air going 70 mph. I've had a lot of crashes along the way. Last night I was discussing pain with a group and what comes with being dedicated to something. When I signed up for downhill skiing I knew there would be pain along the way. We talked about how that relates to real estate. Everyone experiences physical or emotional pain, picking up the phone, that's pain. Without going through a little pain there won't be prosperity. And I apply to my career that it's just part of the deal and it makes success that much sweeter.

DD: So what I hear a lot is, "I know what I need to do so I just need to do it. I don't need a coach. I'm going to just practice on my own." How many coaches did you have?

ES: To not have a coach would be crazy, my coach was always there. One thing I did learn was to always be my best coach. In order to help navigate and learn technique and build the foundation for good skiing, without a coach I would have been lost at sea.

DD: Tell me what you mean by being your own best coach.

ES: It's about knowing yourself and knowing what works for you. If you have 10 different coaches over 10 years and you're pulling in all this information and you can't dissect the information and use what's best for yourself, then it's just too much. Extract the information that's important and applicable to you. Another thing is the power of writing things down. As an athlete, when I wrote my goals down I was much more likely to succeed. One of the things I did before I went to bed was to write my goals down the night before a race or training so that I would wake up with a plan. I would write them on 3 x 5 cards and I would stick them in my helmet so I could pull them out before a race if I got nervous.

DD: It sounds like you are obviously very disciplined and I am too. People always ask me, "Were you born like that?" Were you? Because I know I wasn't.

ES: Well, I think it's a combination of being born like that, having good parenting, and having a goal and looking at something and saying, "I want that but how am I going to get there?" So it becomes process oriented as opposed to goal oriented. It's okay to write your goals down but if that's all you think about then you're going to be lost along the way. So you have to pull back and think about the process. What are all the little steps that will take me where I want to go?

DD: I'm always fascinated with athletes. I'm fascinated with the discipline, the mindset, the pregame warm up, the routine. It's so important to know what your routine is. There's process.

ES: Yes, process and, obviously, a schedule. We had scheduled training sessions, scheduled rest sessions, scheduled video sessions. Everything was scheduled. In some ways it's easy to be part of a team because it gets scheduled for you. Now that I'm in real estate, one of my biggest challenges is schedules.

DD: So Erik, tell us about that.

ES: I'm working with buyers. We have a team. My mom, Marny, focuses on the listings and she's great at it. That phone for her is a lot lighter than it is for me. I would rather go door knock than pick up the phone. My challenge is to leverage what I've done and to prospect in my style and I haven't figured that out yet. Picking up the phone is something that does scare me.

DD: And that's what we talked about yesterday. You don't all have to do it in the same way. For me to say, "You should just cold call." That would be silly because you have so many connections. I'm curious, though, how are you using the pattern of all that discipline to get through the pain of prospecting?

ES: Right now I'm still in the learning phase, so I shadow Kevin, my mom, my dad. I've been around real estate all of my life. I'm trying to learn as much as I can and formulate a plan because I want to make sure

I'm organized and have a plan moving forward, as opposed to just jumping in and going crazy and having to re-structure.

DD: Tell us what is the team going to do this year?

ES: Originally we thought we would hit about $1.5 million in closed commissions, but we've had a pretty good month and I think we're going to do close to $2 million in income. And I just want to talk about competition and inter-office competition. My sport as a ski racer was an individual sport but we traveled and trained as a team. But on race day we were competitors. But we knew every day that we needed each other because if my brother skied fast, that meant I was going to ski faster. If I skied fast, that meant he was going to ski faster. So we used each other to get better and that's a lot like real estate in my opinion, because in real estate you're individuals working in an office and living as a team, but you're competing as individuals. You really can look at your competitors as something that will make you better. If you think of it that way it makes it a little more fun.

DD: Any last thoughts about your successes?

ES: I guess we can talk about the world championships in 2003 and an analogy that you can draw from sports to business. The giant slalom is a two run race and best combined time wins. So after my first run I was in 23rd place with 2 seconds out, which is an eternity. I just relaxed and focused on the fundamentals and went out and in my second run made up over 2 seconds and ended up getting the bronze medal.

DD: I guess the message is that a small shift in skill can change the outcome.

Is It Time For You To Hire A Professional Coach?

Most top professionals have one. If you look at any industry and most professions you will usually find that top performers do have something in common – they all have professional coaches. In fact, some of them have several coaches, and many of them hire coaches at the very beginning of their career and continue in coaching throughout their entire career. I think you would probably agree that those who are coached and held accountable outperform those who are not.

Why Do Those Who Are Coached Out Perform Those Who Are Not In Coaching?

People who are coached by a stellar coach receive insights and guidance that help them find new and better methods of creating the business they need. A coach can be objective and can see the gaps and pitfalls you may miss, and I am sure you would agree the last thing you want to happen is to leave money on the table that should be in your pocket.

Top performers understand that they never arrive, that there is always a next level of mastery, and they know that it just simply isn't possible to know every single thing they would need to know to grow their business rapidly and efficiently. They also know they must stay one step ahead of their competitors at all times and may need resources outside of what they already possess to do so.

After two decades of coaching some of the brightest and best, I find that those who are coached are, for the most part, happier in their business and more confident in their ability. They have a plan, someone to support and encourage them, and someone to hold them accountable to follow through with it.

I personally have several coaches and advisors; an exercise coach, a marketing coach, a financial coach, and a strategy and business development coach. I coach the Excelleum faculty, and they in turn coach each other to share their talent and expertise inside of our organization. Just like you, I am always looking to grow and improve.

My Family Is A Real Estate Family

Unlike some coaching companies whose owners and coaches have never held a real estate license, I have renewed mine for the ninth time. My parents were in real estate, my husband is a 30+ year veteran who is still actively selling, and my twin daughters Taylor and Erika have joined us in the business. I live and breathe real estate every day and so do my veteran coaches who have decades of industry experience. As soon as my daughters passed their real estate tests, I immediately hired multiple coaches from my coaching faculty to work with them to help accelerate their growth and improve their skills.

I started them out on day one with coaches because I believe in coaching and I know that if I want to help them fast track their success, they need the advice and guidance of experts. Coaching is affordable and practical!

> *"Debbie De Grote is amazing, with her expertise and knowledge of the business I have increased my business by over 35%! I will continue to work with Debbie as she has been encouraging, reliable, and her wisdom is priceless! If you are looking to further your real estate career, Debbie is the coach you need to work with to get to the next level!"*
> Lisa Loyd, Realtor, The Stanfield Group – HOM Sotheby's International Realty

Why Do Industry Experts Recommend You Hire A Coach?

Over the years I have heard many experts talk about why real estate agents especially need coaching, so I thought I would share with you a few of their thoughts on the subject.

1) Agents need coaching because there are well over 1.2 million real estate agents in the industry. In other words, the competition is fierce. Even though many agents produce at a very low level, they still grab a few deals here and there, taking away from the opportunities a true professional agent might have captured if there were fewer licensees. Because it is so competitive you need every advantage you can possibly have to close a higher percentage of the prospects you meet.

> *"My name is Boris Kholodov and I'm a real estate broker in Toronto. I reached out to Debbie about a year ago because I was in need of a break through. I had been selling real estate for 14 years, my production was at a standstill, I was complacent. Even though I was successful I really needed to get to that next level, and by creating a strategy that worked for me and by being there every step of the way helping me implement it Debbie managed to get me*

to almost double my average sale price, increase my transaction volume, and therefore more than double my gross commission income. And that's just in one year and she says this is just the beginning. I can't wait to see what's next. Thank you Debbie."
Boris Kholodov, Broker, Royal LePage Real Estate Services, Ltd.

2) Real estate is one of the easiest industries to get into and yet one of the most difficult to succeed in! Think about it... what other profession requires so little training and testing? What other profession does so little to prepare new agents to grow and to help seasoned agents step up to their next level of success? As we all know, simply passing the test does not ensure success. In fact, my book *Secrets of Super Salespeople – Why 80% Fail and How Not to be one of Them,* was inspired by a conversation I had with my daughter Erika.

At the time Erika was still in school and doing part-time transaction coordination for my husband Don. She was preparing to take her real estate test and came home one day and asked me this question, "Mom, why is it that I see perfectly smart and well-dressed people at the real estate office, and then one day they are gone and they never really sell anything? And why is it that there seems to be so many real estate agents everywhere?" She was already beginning to realize that this business might be just a bit tougher than she had imagined.

Another Reason Agents Hire Coaches

3) Once a new or seasoned agent joins an office or company, even the very best company, often the company/management simply doesn't have enough time to spend with each agent to help him or her grow. Often managers are run ragged trying to 'fire fight' to help agents keep deals together, to recruit and provide basic contract training and there just isn't enough time in their day to focus on each agent and give them the time they need.

It's not their fault, it's just that they already have a big job, and quite frankly, may not be skilled at coaching and mentoring because it's not their strength and they haven't been taught how to do so. They may also not have the expertise in the particular areas an agent wants to grow into.

A Few More Thoughts To Consider...

4) Real estate is one of the few industries where veterans, experts, and top producers are typically not willing to share their knowledge because they fear they will educate their competition. It is very difficult for new agents to find a mentor.

5) Regarding the veteran agents, no matter how good they are, if they don't stay on top of new developments and if they aren't operating on the cutting edge, they will be branded a dinosaur and left behind.

All of these reasons are exactly why industry professionals who have aggressive growth goals know that they need a coach. They need someone they can rely on who knows them, has their back, and has a high level of expertise to help them be all they can be.

It is also evident that today's consumer is so much more savvy than just a few years ago. The internet has empowered the consumer with information they did not have access to in the past. The average seller today interviews 3-5 agents before choosing one. Even buyers are jumping on the bandwagon of aggressively vetting the agent they choose to work with.

Because sellers and buyers are more selective than ever before, it is absolutely critical that you be able to set yourself apart from the masses. You must be a skilled communicator, a chameleon with great sales versatility, a strategist, a market expert, and a tech and marketing wizard, and you must be highly organized. Wow! It's a tall order, I know. That is exactly why you need to hire us to coach you.

> *"As a top producing mortgage professional, I appreciate the fresh insight that I get weekly on my coaching calls with Debbie and her team. She is nothing short of a genius in this industry and has parlayed her real world experience into powerful and implementable ideas. She has a knack for solving problems with simple solutions. My business has nearly doubled in the 2 years that I have been coaching with Debbie. While I would like to take full credit, I know that the team at Excelleum has contributed greatly to my success. "*
>
> Andrew Soss, Branch Manager, Guaranteed Rate

In the past, real estate really was a personality-driven business. If a potential client loved you they would hire you. Personality will no longer be the deciding factor in how the consumer chooses an agent. There will need to be substance and it will need to be clear to them why the agent they are choosing is different from the rest. If you cannot differentiate yourself clearly from the competition then there is only one thing you can do to compete – cut commission – not a great way to win business!

It's No Longer Possible To Sell On Personality

So if you can't rely on your charming personality anymore to attract and win business what can you rely on? You need systems and skills. You need systems for how you create leads, how you capture and convert the leads, systems to manage and service the client, a system for hiring staff, and systems for training and holding them accountable. You also need the highest level of skill possible to maximize productivity and keep it all spinning.

It is true that most real estate agents are not equipped with the skills and training to build a systematic business. It's not because they aren't smart and it's not because they aren't educated, as many have Masters Degrees or more.

The reality is that 90% of people coming into the business were trained in a previous career to do process work. What I mean by that is the company or business they came from already had systems in place for them to follow. Once they get into real estate they are lost because they don't know how to build their own systems. When agents hire us to coach them their top priority is "help me build my systems!"

Maybe you are thinking…

> "I know what I need to do I just need to do it."

Forgive me for being blunt and I don't mean to be rude but I do have to ask, how do you know that you know what you need to do? What I mean is this– you don't know what you don't know, right?

It's just not possible for one person to drag around a wheelbarrow big enough to hold everything they might need to know and do to succeed. When you hire a coach, and especially when that coach has a head coach and a strong coaching faculty to draw on, suddenly everything becomes easier. The vision and the path to get to the vision become clear.

Another reason to consider coaching is this: everything today moves at such a rapid pace – technology, social media, new tools, etc. Sellers especially want next generation strategies. It's simply impossible for one person alone to stay on top of all of the new developments and be able to articulate them to a potential customer. This is why you need a coach and a community of elite agents to associate with.

However, maybe you don't want to be coached. If that is the case, then you shouldn't join us. You see, it's not my goal in this report to convince you to do something you don't want to do. Maybe you are 100% happy with the money you are currently earning and the level of success, financial freedom, and quality of life that you have. Are you?

If we are honest with each other, wouldn't it be fair to say that you clearly know what you can earn without a coach? So if you are okay with making what you have made so far, then you don't need a coach.

> *"Myself and my team have been coaching with Debbie for over a year now. In that time, our production/revenue has increased 27% and we are currently number 1 in market share in all of our markets. This is directly attributable to Debbie's coaching. She keeps us on a uniformed message, has helped round out our business model and made us more efficient. I would highly recommend Debbie De Grote to anyone who wants efficient, smart and innovative coaching. Thanks Debbie, for all your help and guidance!!!"*
> Kevin Kelly/The Kelly Team, Area Manager, Chicago Title

Again, if you can say, "I am 100% satisfied with all aspects of my life and business," then you don't need a coach. If, however, you are not 100% satisfied, then you should strongly consider hiring us to coach you.

There could be another reason you shouldn't hire us to coach you– you simply are not motivated.

If you are not motivated to improve, then you shouldn't hire us, because when you hire us to coach you my team is all in. I have an incredibly dedicated group of veterans in the industry standing by to help. They coach because they are passionate about helping you and they are very, very good at it. But if you don't want to grow then we really can't help you. I hope that by now you are realizing that you do want to grow, that you do need help, and that you can benefit from coaching.

I want to give you a few more logical reasons to consider just to make your decision that much easier.

Why Hire Us To Coach You?

- You want to dramatically grow your business, team, or organization. Did you know that 99% of the top 10% of top producers in the industry are strong listing agents? We absolutely coach you to exponentially increase your listing inventory and then help you more efficiently convert, delegate, and manage the buyer leads the listings create.
- You need a strategy to help maximize growth without sacrificing your quality of life.
- There are gaps in your current skills that must be fixed for you to win at a higher level.
- You need systems and structure to your business.
- You need help to eliminate the chaos that overwhelms you.
- You need someone who understands who you are and can provide the encouragement and support you need.
- Maybe you have tried coaching in the past and it didn't work for you and that is causing you to hesitate now. I wonder, what went wrong? Maybe you weren't coachable, or maybe you just had the wrong coach focusing on the wrong things? It's probably the latter – you had the wrong coach. That is why everyday clients are coming to us, because they know we can actually deliver what others only promise. We can and do deliver results.
- Maybe you want to break into a new price point or market. This is a terrific way to expand your business and many of our clients excel in the luxury and ultra-luxury market. If this is your goal, it will be critical that we help you identify the luxury segment to tap into, and help you upgrade your tools and presentation to meet the demands of the luxury seller and the very tough competitors you will face in this arena.
- You need help with putting challenging transactions together. (I am not surprised because it's just a fact that today's transactions are very, very complex and that's exactly why I only hire coaches with decades of industry experience so that they can help you through tough negotiations.)

"I have been working with my Excelleum coach since December 2014, so only for a few months, but in that short time I have found Gus to be invaluable. He's reshaped my thinking about pricing listings. He's been someone to turn to for advice, both broad direction for general questions and specific to-do's for challenging transactions. After nearly 13 years of selling real estate, I feel like

I've found a mentor, someone who, over time, will guide me to the next level. Thanks, Gus!"

Roz Essner, Realtor, Re/Max Select One

- You are tired of going at it alone. I understand real state can be a lonely business, especially with more and more agents working from home.

Do any of these reasons above apply to you? If so, then please read on! Another question I am sometimes asked is this, "Do you guarantee the results?" No, we cannot guarantee the results because we cannot force you to do the work. Clients who join us in the coaching and do the work have explosive growth, we have clients who have doubled and tripled their business. Of course we cannot guarantee those results for you because only you can decide what you will or will not do.

If you don't believe we can help you, re-read the testimonials in this report and on our website. Or reach out to us and we can share many, many more!

There are some guarantees we can give you. We will get to know you. We will match you with the right coach. We will be all in to deliver the coaching and training you need to get you where you want to be. Our outstanding retention rates and raving reviews from our amazing clients are proof that we deliver results. We even coach clients that do $100, $200, $400 million in volume. You must realize that producers at this level wouldn't hire us and stay with us if the coaching wasn't stellar, would they?

Let's talk for a minute about what the coaching experience will be like, and more specifically what your coaching experience with Excelleum will be like, because we are different.

"Aren't we fortunate?! Finally a coach philosophy out there that is not a "one size fits all"! Debbie De Grote and her Excelleum Team are such a breath of fresh air for our Real Estate industry! I, as a Broker/Office Manager, and some my agents have been coached by Debbie for about 6 months now. Every call, meeting, webinar or just an email from Debbie are loaded with great information, new strategies, out of the box approaches to grow our business. Furthermore, Debbie's NLP skills wow me with the best scripts! From a few words to break the ice, to a powerful closing! Best coach ever!"

Beth Hale, Manager, Berkshire Hathaway Home Services

What we do differently than the rest is this: we see each client for their uniqueness – their unique market, their unique talents and skills, and their unique definition of success. We do not believe in a 'one-size fits all' approach to coaching. Our strategic and in-depth coaching and consulting style means that we must have only the most seasoned coaches on our staff... and we do!

> *"I have found Excelleum to be very approachable and helpful. Debbie always listens and makes great suggestions for me. I love that she does not say, 'You must do xyz this way ONLY.' She guides me to what I need to do but in a way that I eventually do even though it scares me. I am really pleased to find someone who coaches in the Tai Chi way. She goes with and then guides to the best way. Thank you Debbie for this type of coaching. It is very different to the 'YOU MUST' way where I decide to do it but then I hit a brick wall of fear and don't 'DO'."*
> Audrey Goodbar, Century 21 Realty Masters

We Have Some Of The Most Experienced and Talented Coaches In The Industry!

Our coaches on average have 30+ years of experience in all aspects of the industry and they are then trained extensively by me to ensure that they can provide exactly what the client needs when they need it. Because I am passionate about coaching, sales, and seeing our clients grow, I will not hire anyone who is not outstanding to be a coach on my team! Once they join me I continue to train them so that they can be all that they can be for you!

While each call is customized to fit the clients' needs, we do have a very systematic approach to the coaching process. Let me walk you through it now.

Our 5 Step Process

Step 1: We conduct a very thorough analysis to determine exactly where you are in your business right now.

Step 2: We examine your goals and help you define the vision you have of how you want your business to evolve.

Step 3: We analyze the gaps in your business that may be preventing you from achieving your goal. We call this the "business overhaul."

Step 4: We create for you and with you, a customized success blueprint that will give you a clear path to follow.

Step 5: We hold you accountable to stay the course and help you make necessary adjustments along the way.

Often our clients see explosive growth after just a few sessions – some experience 25%, 35%, 50% growth when coaching with us. Not everyone grows at such a rapid rate, because it depends on the focus and the drive of each individual, and it also depends on their own personal goals. Some want to grow their sales, some want to build a team, and some simply want to refine the business they have to improve their quality of life.

How Is My Coach Selected?

I love it when I am asked this question, because to me this is a very critical aspect of the coaching process, and yet most coaching companies randomly assign you to whoever needs or wants a client.

As I mentioned, we begin by getting to know you, helping you select the right program, having you take your DISC assessment and complete a Business Needs Analysis. I thoroughly review all the information and if I have questions, I will reach out to you before I make the final selection.

I am the only person who matches you to your coach and I ensure that it is a perfect match or I will re-match you at no cost to you for that very first call, if you are not 100% satisfied. At Excelleum you have the unique opportunity to work with more than one coach if needed for areas of specialty you may want to tap into. You can always reach out to me. All clients have my personal email address and phone number.

Let's talk a little bit more about the results and the experience you can expect. I have already shared with you the percentage of growth our clients often achieve. However, I think we both know there is more to growth and achievement than just transactions. This is why in our very first call with you we will ask you to describe your vision for your business and your life. Once we are clear on your vision we can work to create the path to get you there. Our job is to accurately assess where you are today vs. where you want to be tomorrow and to help you close the gap to get there.

I recently read an article online that stated that today 68% of real estate agents hire a coach and that this number is growing daily. We know that each and every day the market becomes more competitive. Coaching can give you the edge you need to beat the competition, find new opportunities, and close more of the prospects you meet.

At Excelleum our goal is to help you achieve your goals by truly working smarter, not harder. We see you for who you are, a uniquely talented person, and we help you maximize your talents.

I hope that you have found this section helpful. I hope that you will take the next step and reach out to us today! If you are seriously considering coaching, let us know by registering for a complimentary business strategy call at www.businessstrategycall.com.

On this call we will:
- Get to know you
- Help you identify the gaps and opportunities in your business
- Answer your questions about the coaching program you are interested in

It's a process! Now that you know quite a bit about us, I want to ask you a few questions and give you a few things to consider.

What really are you risking by hiring us to coach you? When you consider the amount of your average commission check most likely 1-3 closings would more than cover the cost of coaching for 6, 9, 12 months or more. Do you really believe that we couldn't help you at least earn enough extra to cover the cost? Can you imagine when you have access to my talented coaches, scripts, videos, virtual campus, and resource center how much you can accomplish? Couldn't you without a doubt pick up 5, 10, or even 15 listings? Honestly, there really is no limit to what you could do. Only you will decide how high you go.

So what are you really risking?

What are all the things you feel you could truly gain by joining coaching?

When you think about it, aren't you the best investment you could make? It's very common that agents throw a lot of money at marketing, and yet 80% of marketing dollars are wasted producing little or no return. Or they attend conventions and sign up for all sorts of services, and then don't use them or don't know how to properly use them. Most agents waste hundreds and thousands of dollars per month on stuff! I will ask you again, "Aren't you your best investment?"

I had a crazy thought as I sat down to write this chapter. I thought, what if we brought all of the real estate agents in North America to the Grand Canyon and we put those in coaching on one side of the canyon and those not in coaching on the other side. Which group would ultimately make the most money? Which side would you be on?

I get that by now you know I am trying to sell you on hiring us to coach you. Of course I am, because I am confident that we can help you! I also know that you are probably thinking about the cost of the coaching, maybe even worrying that you cannot afford it. Can you afford not to do it?

When you think about hiring us to coach you, you know exactly what it will cost, but what we don't know is what will the cost be if you don't hire us? How much money and how many possibilities will you be leaving on the table? If you are telling me that you want to do it and you know you need it, but you just can't afford it, then I am telling you that these are all of the reasons that you must find the money to join. The fact that you do not have the money you need to do the things you want to do is not an acceptable situation, is it?

If you can't afford the very reasonable coaching fee then there are probably other things in your life you want that you can't afford. Aren't you tired of being denied what you deserve?

I wonder what the competitors in your market would tell you do to. They would tell you not to join, because the last thing they would want you to have is an advantage over them, the advantage that coaching with us will give you.

For the services we provide and the talent we bring to the table, our prices actually should be much higher. The value of what we give is so much greater than what we charge. So why aren't they higher? Well, if they were you wouldn't pay and then we wouldn't have the chance to work with you. We know that once you join us you will do what most of our clients do, become a client for life and move up the ladder to our higher level coaching programs. That's exactly why we are realistic, patient, and understanding.

I read this great quote the other day, "You dominate your thinking by clearly defining what it is you want. Then you must define what you are truly willing to do to get it!"

> *"Debbie's coaching is constantly motivating me to strive to take my business to the next level. While working with her I have seen my communication skills grow, ultimately enhancing my ability to interact with and turn my prospects into clients and close deals. The techniques that I've learned have not only helped increase my sales and bring success in the business world, but they have applied to my personal life and relationships as well. She's knowledgeable, passionate, energetic, and she genuinely cares about my success!"*
> Chad M. Engle, Realtor Associate, Realty One Group

So what do you want? Are you willing to do whatever it takes to get there? If you are, then it's time you make a commitment to hire us to help you get where you want to be. I know you may be thinking "I have to think it over", "I have to talk to my spouse", or "I have to wait until my next closing." These are all excuses, right? We hear them all the time. Do you know what else we hear all the time? "I wish you would have made me join coaching last year! I have lost so much time and money by being stuck in my indecision."

I don't want this to happen to you! You deserve to be as successful and as happy as you can possibly be. I want you to understand the power of saying "Yes!" to yourself.

Don't you need a total transformation...a complete breakthrough? Haven't you already tried to go it alone? It's not really working is it? Remember, you are not alone. This is not unusual because this is a hard business. Remember too, all top athletes, performers, and superstars in business have coaches. It is simply what it takes to get to the next level. One of the most consistent characteristics of the most successful people in life is this: they possess the ability to make decisions. For example, if you are struggling to make this very important decision to invest in yourself and your future, could this be why sometimes you may struggle leading your clients to make decisions? I want to encourage you now to make a decision and take the following actions:

#1 READ THIS CHAPTER AGAIN. Maybe you missed something or you just need to hear it again.

#2 WRITE DOWN YOUR QUESTIONS. Write down any questions you have and we will answer them.

#3 REGISTER FOR YOUR COMPLIMENTARY SESSION. Give us a call at 714.625.5226 or visit www.businessstrategycall.com now to register for your complimentary session.

Don't wait any longer. Give us a call today – it's time to move forward.

We look forward to welcoming you in!

Strategic Questions for All Present and Future Teams

In order to build a bigger, busier, and more profitable team, even if it is your team members who will become busier and not you, it is vital that you develop the right strategy. The right strategy begins by a process of rigorous introspection.

What is your unique selling proposition? Maybe it's you! It could be your talent, inspiration, and mentoring, along with the coaching and training you may choose to provide. It is vital that you are able to define and sell the value of the benefits that you bring to the table.

You must plan to make the appropriate profit so you are properly compensated for all of your time and energy invested. You must also resolve issues of compensation as firmly as possible. If you start team members too high on their compensation plan and then are forced to reduce compensation, you will have a recipe for retention related disaster.

More people does not necessarily make for a better or more profitable team! Having lots of people working for you with little profit is merely a distraction and a drain on your energy. If you do not see potential and they are not making you money, they cannot stay.

I, therefore, encourage you to take a few minutes and answer the following list of extensive questions. Discuss them with your broker or manager, and contact us if you want some additional help and advice.

1. Why am I building a team? What do I want? What do I need?
2. What are my first priorities in the formation of a team?
3. What do I want my team to look like? How many people? What responsibilities will they have?
4. Can my business support an administrative person, a buyer specialist and/or a listing specialist? Can I provide sufficient leads?
5. Should I name my organization a team, a group, a partnership, or "blank" and associates? List the pros and cons of each choice.
6. Do I possess stronger leadership, management, or selling skills?
7. Am I prepared financially to fund the team's creation and growth?

8. Am I prepared to ensure that every team member is effective and totally focused on their respective responsibility?
9. Do I have systems and templates in place to allow new team members to jump start their productivity and to follow protocols?
10. Do I have a checklist for every transaction to ensure superior customer service and prevent important tasks from falling through the cracks?
11. Do I have training/apprenticeship protocols in place and a plan for continual education and team service training?
12. Do I have a career growth opportunity roadmap for team members?
13. Do I plan to use non-competes, non-disclosures and/or confidentiality agreements? If yes, do I have templates for them?
14. Do I have a template for proposed income plans?
15. Do I have a template for my team brand and my marketing plan, and are they consistent and compatible?
16. How will I track revenue, expenses, and profitability? Am I comfortable using a profit and loss statement?
17. How will the team respond to/follow-up/divide leads?
18. What expenses will be covered by the team leader and by the team member?
19. What is the post-closing follow-up plan to stay in contact with clients and to measure client satisfaction?
20. What are the team's lead generation expectations and resources?
21. How will the team utilize technology and systems to gain leverage?
22. How will I screen team applicants and measure their suitability?
23. Have I thought about succession planning?
24. Am I prepared to inspect what I expect?
25. Is my present company supportive of my starting or further growing my team?
26. What contact management system will I use?
27. Who will design my team website?
28. How will I break down internal versus external coaching?
29. Will our team's marketing be team exclusive versus from the company?
30. How often will our team meet and what will team meetings consist of?
31. How will I structure compensation for my team?
32. How do I intend to further the career development of team members?

33. Will I use a personality related diagnostic assessment such as the DISC?
34. What will my team do that other teams also do, but will do better?
35. What will my team do that no one else does?

Okay, now that you have answered the questions and are still gung ho and certain it's what you want to do, there are four areas that will need some serious attention before you proceed. These four areas are where we find our coaching clients often need the most help.

1) You will need to develop an overarching and comprehensive strategy and then constantly work to improve on it if you want to create and sustain a highly successful team.
2) You will need to develop a strategic approach for staffing, organizational development, division of labor, compensation, legalities, selection, and career development of team members.
3) You will need to outline best practices and then conduct an ongoing examination of what methods of success are being employed from top real estate teams across North America. This includes team accountability and a high emphasis on brand and marketing differentiation. You need to be able to out innovate as well as out compete.
4) Growth and secession strategies, preparing your team or group for secession (successfully withdrawing and passing your team on for enumeration). In *The E-Myth Revisited*, Michael Gerber says, "The only reason you build a business is to sell it." Even if you never choose to sell, you still want to build a business that is such a turnkey operation that buyers would be lining up to buy into it or buy it outright from you.

What are the questions team leaders often ask us as we coach them?

Q: How do I hire the right people?
Q: How can I be the type of leader that inspires loyalty and team cohesiveness?
Q: How much should I produce personally?
Q: How much of my duties and activities should I delegate?
Q: How are other team leaders compensating their team members?
Q: How much do I need to differentiate my team from my company?
Q: How much of my company's branding should I employ vs. my own?
Q: Should I be looking for new or seasoned team members?

Q: Should I consolidate my teams production as part of my personal numbers to better establish my teams local visibility and to increase my credibility and competitive edge as the rain maker?

Q: Should I develop a team of specialists or a team of generalists?

Q: Should I assign geographical areas of concentration or encourage my team members to define their own markets according to their interests?

Q: What should be the chronology of team hires?

The rest will need to be addressed on a one on one basis, by potentially putting you together with one of my coaches. Because, as we started the book by stating, no two agents, teams, groups , companies or brands are alike, and, therefore, each question needs to be carefully examined to insure the right recommendations are made for the vision you have, the strengths you have, and the market you are in.

Acknowledgements

This book could not have been written without the invaluable assistance of my co-author Allan Dalton. He is one of the most brilliant people I have ever met and a priceless member of my coaching faculty.

I also would be remiss not to thank my daughter, Taylor De Grote, for her research and very contemporary insights.

Most importantly, this book owes its existence to all those interviewed who were gracious enough to share their experiences and advice. I hope you reward them with your thanks and your referrals, because they are truly amazing!

Speaking of amazing, I want to thank my coaches for their dedication and commitment to excellence. Thank you also to all of our wonderful clients who allow us to assist in their success.

P.S. Thank you to my staff for assisting us in this labor of love. Without you we couldn't have pulled it all together.

About the Authors

Debbie De Grote sold her first home at the age of 18, while still in high school. From that time Debbie continued to expand her skills and growt

h in the sales industry. Debbie's personal production was consistently between 12 - 15 units per month on average. During her tenure with Century 21 she was ranked the Number 1 Real Estate Agent in Los Angeles and Orange County and Top 10 internationally.

Debbie was consistently asked to coach and train other sales professionals to achieve their potential. After nearly two decades of front lines selling Debbie became a full-time coach and business consultant. She has coached some of the biggest names and largest companies not only in the real estate industry, but across a wide-range of industries including; title, mortgage, insurance, and nutraceuticals, among others.

Debbie has a unique knack for inspiring and leading other people to the highest levels of success across multiple industries. When asked about what she does that is unique for her clients, Debbie replied, "I don't implement 'one size fits all' coaching and training programs. Instead, I invest the time needed to learn and understand every client, every company, and their specific training needs. Then I customize a program that is uniquely their own. I immerse myself in their culture and become a part of their team." Debbie's passion is the Art of Selling and helping her clients achieve their sales, business, and life goals. Debbie is a published author of numerous materials and publications and is constantly studying new techniques.

Allan Dalton is the Former President of the Move Inc. Real Estate Division and CEO of Realtor.com. He was named by The National Association of Realtors© as one of the real estate industry's 25 Most Influential Thought Leaders.

For 20 years Dalton was co-owner and President of a 32-office New Jersey brokerage and, after selling his company to Realogy, became a SR VP of NRT, and then EVP of Coldwell Banker New England.

Dalton, a former Boston Celtics draft choice, is also credited with creating National Marketing systems for *Better Homes and Gardens*, ERA, Century 21 and Coldwell Banker NRT.

Dalton is the author of *Leveraging your Links, and Creating Real Estate Connections,* and is the co-founder of the Top 5 in Real Estate and Town Advisor.com, and served as Chief Marketing Officer for RIS Media. Dalton presently runs AllanDaltonConsulting, where he consults numerous industry related brokerages and service providers, and is a member of The Excelleum Coaching & Consulting faculty

Allan Dalton, a frequent real estate convention speaker, lives with his wife of 43 years, Carol, in Westlake Village, California and they are very proud of their nine grandchildren.

CPSIA information can be obtained
at www.ICGtesting.com
Printed in the USA
FSOW01n1951301216
28983FS